Tiny Food Party

TINY FOOD PARTY!

bite-size recipes for miniature meals

By Teri Lyn Fisher
& Jenny Park

QUIRK BOOKS
PHILADELPHIA

To Dexti, Tigger, and Napoleon.
Thank you for always lending a paw.

Library of Congress Cataloging in Publication Number: 2011946056

ISBN: 978-1-59474-581-2

Printed in China

Typeset in Neutraface No. 2

Designed by Katie Hatz
Photography by Teri Lyn Fisher
Production management by John J. McGurk

Quirk Books
215 Church Street
Philadelphia, PA 19106
www.quirkbooks.com

10 9 8 7 6 5

CONTENTS

INTRODUCTION

Your parents may have taught you never to play with your food, but in this book we encourage it. Well-crafted finger foods beat cheese and crackers or veggies and dip any day. In a world where bigger is better, we think tiny is terrific. We've taken big ideas and shrunk them down into bite-size appetizers that are fun and easy to make.

Food and cooking don't have to be stuffy or fussy. Throwing a party should be exactly that—a party! It should be easy and fun to put together, with a minimal amount of stress. So we created a cookbook filled with unique recipes and beautiful photographs to help make your party awesome. Whether you're cooking for a bunch of carnivores or a group of vegetarians, we've got you covered. We hope this book inspires you to get into the kitchen and get the party started, because there's not much that can compare to a get-together filled with great food, booze, music, and friends.

Chapter 1

TINY SNACK PARTY!

Adorable Appetizers

Bite-Size
CAPRESE SKEWERS

makes 24

Everyone's had caprese salad before, but not like this! These pop-in-your-mouth cherry tomato versions are the perfect way to enjoy the flavors of Italy.

BALSAMIC GLAZE

⅔ cup balsamic vinegar*
¼ cup light brown sugar, packed

SALAD

24 heirloom cherry tomatoes
24 small mozzarella balls
3 sprigs basil
24 cocktail picks

Use a smooth, good-quality balsamic, such as Maletti or Fini.

1. For the glaze, place vinegar and sugar in a small saucepan over medium-low heat. Stir and simmer for about 45 minutes, until the mixture reduces by half and thickens slightly. Let cool. *{Tip: The glaze will continue to thicken as it cools.}*
2. Using a sharp knife, cut tomatoes in half and mozzarella balls in thirds. Sandwich a slice of mozzarella and a basil leaf between each tomato half. Skewer with a cocktail pick, drizzle with glaze, and serve.

The balsamic glaze can be made a day or two ahead, but the skewers are best assembled shortly before serving; otherwise, the basil leaves may brown. Put your party guests to work putting them together!

Two-Bite

SAVORY SCONES

makes 24

These savory scones are filled with flavors of the Mediterranean: sun-dried tomatoes, feta, and fresh herbs. They're a delicious and filling snack, whether plated with afternoon brunch, packed into lunchboxes, or served at happy hour.

- 2 cups all-purpose flour
- 2 tablespoons sugar
- 1½ teaspoons baking powder
- ½ teaspoon baking soda
- 1 teaspoon salt
- ½ cup (1 stick) cold butter, cut into small cubes
- ⅔ cup diced sun-dried tomatoes
- ⅔ cup crumbled feta cheese
- 1 tablespoon minced fresh thyme
- 2 teaspoons minced fresh oregano
- 2 teaspoons minced fresh rosemary
- 1 teaspoon black pepper
- ½ cup buttermilk
- ¼ cup heavy cream

1. Preheat oven to 375°F. Line a baking sheet with parchment paper.
2. In a large bowl, sift together flour, sugar, baking powder, baking soda, and salt. Cut butter into the flour mixture until it is completely incorporated and mixture has a fine, mealy texture. Add sun-dried tomatoes, cheese, herbs, and pepper and stir to combine. Fold in buttermilk and stir just until dough comes together.
3. Divide dough into 4 disks. Cut each disk into 6 wedges. Place wedges onto the prepared baking sheet.
4. Lightly brush the top of each wedge with heavy cream and bake for 18 to 20 minutes, or until scones puff up and the tops just start to brown. Serve warm.

Try baking bite-size scones with your favorite herbs and cheeses. The secret to scones of any size is this: don't overwork the dough, or your scones will come out dense and tough instead of light and buttery.

Mini KIMCHI DEVILED EGGS

makes 48

Mini deviled eggs may be among the best appetizers ever invented. A bit of kimchi and a candied-bacon topping add a wonderful *umami* twist to this classic American hors d'oeuvre.

DEVILED QUAIL EGGS

24 hard-boiled quail eggs, peeled and halved lengthwise
¼ cup chopped kimchi*
2 tablespoons thinly sliced green onions
2 tablespoons mayonnaise (regular or light)
Salt and pepper, to taste

TOPPING

¼ cup Candied Bacon (page 110)

**Available at Asian markets and many major supermarkets, this beloved Korean staple has a sweet yet sour flavor. It's made from crunchy fresh Napa cabbage brined then soaked in a rich and fiery chili-garlic sauce.*

1. Separate yolks from whites; set hollowed whites aside. Place yolks in a mixing bowl and mash together; add kimchi, green onions, and mayonnaise, season with salt and pepper, and stir to combine.
2. Fill each white with about 1 teaspoon of filling and top with a small sprinkle of candied bacon. Serve.

If you're not a fan of kimchi or you just love deviled eggs, try these tasty variations. For Spicy Deviled Eggs, add 1 tablespoon hot sauce and 2 teaspoons seeded and minced jalapeño to the filling. Mix ½ teaspoon cayenne pepper into the brown sugar before candying the bacon. For Herbed Deviled Eggs, add 1 teaspoon Dijon mustard, ½ teaspoon minced tarragon, and ½ teaspoon thinly sliced chives to the filling.

A Small Secret

QUAIL EGGS

Quail eggs are easier to come by than you might think. You can find them at gourmet grocery stores and Asian supermarkets, as well as at some farmers' markets. Cook them as you would chicken eggs, but with shorter cooking times. Allow them to cool before peeling.

QUAIL EGG BOILING CHART

SOFT BOIL:	2 minutes
MEDIUM BOIL:	3 to 4 minutes
HARD BOIL:	5 minutes

Deep-fried quail eggs are crunchy on the outside and soft on the inside—perfect for garnishing salads or Itty-Bitty Bloody Marys (page 136). Simply peel and roll hard- or soft-boiled quail eggs in plain Italian bread crumbs until completely coated. Deep-fry for 2 to 3 minutes, or until crispy and golden brown. The trick is to ensure they are totally coated so they don't burst when fried.

A Little Menu

TINY BBQ/PICNIC

Whether it's warm and beautiful outside or you just want it to be, here's one of our favorite menus for barbecues and picnics. Served on trays, these eats are easy to nibble without utensils.

Potato Salad Bites 19

Potato salad made with crumbled bacon, caramelized onions, green onion, and a spicy whole-grain mustard sauce, spooned into crispy baked wonton cups

Jalapeño and Cheddar Corn Sticks 47

Sweet cornmeal batter with spicy jalapeños and sharp cheddar cheese, baked in mini corn stick pans and served with a drizzle of honey

BBQ Pulled Pork Sandwiches 63

Pulled pork tossed in Homemade BBQ Sauce with chopped peanuts, topped with an apple cider vinegar coleslaw, and served in Hawaiian rolls

Corn Dogs 69

Little smokeys, skewered onto toothpicks and dipped in corn dog batter with crumbled bacon and served with ketchup and yellow mustard

Mac 'n' Cheese Bites 85

Creamy mac 'n' cheese cut into small triangles, coated in panko bread crumbs, and deep-fried

Fried Apple Pies 130

Three-inch pies stuffed with apple filling, fried hot, and served with a drizzle of Vanilla Icing

Ginger-Mint Lemonades 149

Sweet bourbon mixed with fresh-squeezed lemonade and fresh Ginger Simple Syrup, stirred with muddled mint and served as shooters

Tiny POTATO SALAD BITES

makes 24

Baked wonton cups not only add great crunch, they're also a fantastic way to neatly serve this popular side dish sans silverware. Our salad is made with creamy red potatoes, sweet caramelized onions, and salty crumbled bacon, all tossed together with a spicy mustard sauce and scooped into crispy baked wonton cups.

POTATO SALAD

1 pound baby red potatoes,* quartered
2 tablespoons unsalted butter
1 medium yellow onion, thinly sliced (about 2 cups)
½ teaspoon sugar
½ cup mayonnaise (regular or light)
¼ cup whole grain mustard
1 tablespoon apple cider vinegar
Salt and pepper, to taste
1 cup crumbled bacon, plus more for garnish (from about 9 strips)
2 green onions, thinly sliced, plus more for garnish
2 teaspoons crushed red pepper flakes

WONTON CUPS

24 square wonton wrappers

**For Southern-style smashed potato salad, swap red-skinned potatoes for a starchy variety, like russet.*

1. In a large pot, cover potatoes with water. Bring to a boil and cook until potatoes are fork-tender, 15 to 20 minutes. Drain and place in a mixing bowl.
2. To caramelize onions, melt butter in a skillet over medium-high heat. Add onions and sauté for 3 minutes. Reduce heat to low and sprinkle sugar and 2 tablespoons water over top. Stirring frequently, cook onions for 35 to 40 minutes, or until they have wilted and are sweetened. Transfer to a cutting board, chop roughly, and add to potatoes.
3. In a small bowl, whisk together mayonnaise, mustard, and vinegar. Season with salt and pepper. Pour over potatoes and gently stir. Add the remaining potato salad ingredients and carefully fold together until fully combined. Refrigerate salad for at least 6 hours.
4. Preheat oven to 350°F. Coat the inside of a nonstick mini muffin tin with cooking spray. Nestle 1 wonton wrapper into each muffin cup and lightly spray each wrapper. Bake for 6 to 8 minutes, or until crisp and golden brown. Remove cups from pan, transfer to a cooling rack, and let cool completely. To serve, scoop 2 tablespoons of potato salad into each cup. Garnish with green onions and crumbled bacon.

Baked wonton cups are a great party trick. Fill them with scoops of your favorite salads for a finger-food snack.

Mini CRAB CAKES

makes 48

This crispy, bite-size version of an American favorite is nicely paired with a zesty, easy-to-make roasted red pepper aioli.

1. Preheat oven to 375°F.
2. In a large bowl, combine crabmeat, cream cheese, and mayonnaise. Gently fold in the peppers, corn, chives, egg white, and salt and pepper.
3. For the crust, in a small bowl stir to combine bread crumbs, melted butter, chives, and Parmesan. Scoop 1 teaspoon of crust mixture into each cup of a lightly greased nonstick mini muffin tin. Press down gently to form an even layer.
4. Drop about 2 tablespoons of crab mixture into each cup and sprinkle with the remaining crust mixture. Bake for 15 to 20 minutes, or until crab cakes are golden brown and hold together. Serve warm with Roasted Red Pepper Aioli for dipping.

For cute little sandwiches, spread aioli on mini hamburger buns or slider rolls. Top with the crab cakes and mixed greens.

CRAB CAKES

1 pound lump crabmeat*
4 ounces cream cheese, softened
2 tablespoons mayonnaise (regular or light)
3/4 cup minced pimento peppers
1/2 cup frozen corn, thawed
3 tablespoons thinly sliced chives
1 egg white, lightly beaten
Salt and pepper, to taste

CRUST

1 cup panko bread crumbs
3 tablespoons unsalted butter, melted
2 tablespoons thinly sliced chives
1 tablespoon grated Parmesan cheese

About 1/2 cup Roasted Red Pepper Aioli (page 22)

* *For a less expensive but equally delicious option, replace half of the lump crab with claw meat.*

⟼ ROASTED RED PEPPER AIOLI ⟻

makes about $^3/_4$ cup

Making your own condiments from scratch might seem unnecessarily fussy—until you realize how delicious the results can be. This flavorful aioli (essentially, fancy mayonnaise) is perfect for spreading on sandwiches like Little Lamb Sliders (page 66) or as a dipping sauce for Mini Crab Cakes (page 20).

$^1/_2$ cup mayonnaise (regular or light)
$^1/_2$ cup roughly chopped roasted red bell peppers
2 garlic cloves, roughly chopped
Zest and juice of 1 lemon
Salt and pepper, to taste

1. Put mayonnaise, bell peppers, garlic, and lemon in a food processor or blender. Pulse until smooth. Taste, season with salt and pepper, and serve.

Aioli is easy to adapt to a world of flavors. Delicious variations of this recipe include Roasted Garlic Aioli (add 5 roasted garlic cloves, smashed), Lemon Aioli (add the juice of $^1/_2$ lemon, zest of 1 lemon, and 1 garlic clove), or Green Onion and Caper Aioli (add 2 tablespoons capers, 1 green onion, and 1 tablespoon lemon juice).

⟼ BUTTERMILK RANCH SAUCE ⟻

makes about $^1/_2$ cup

This creamy sauce is a cinch to make. It's perfect for dunking crispy hot One-Bite "Onion" Rings (page 25) or—let's be honest—anything fried.

$^1/_3$ cup mayonnaise (regular or light)
3 tablespoons buttermilk (regular or low fat)
1 teaspoon fresh lemon juice
1$^1/_2$ tablespoons minced flat-leaf parsley
1 tablespoon thinly sliced chives
$^1/_2$ teaspoon minced dill
$^1/_2$ teaspoon dry mustard
Salt and pepper, to taste

1. In a medium bowl, whisk mayonnaise, buttermilk, lemon juice, parsley, chives, dill, and mustard until thoroughly combined. Season with salt and pepper. Cover and refrigerate until ready to serve.

A Little Menu

QUICK AND EASY PARTY FOOD

Whip up these super simple, delicious recipes when you're short on time. Easy peasy!

Caprese Skewers 10

Small mozzarella balls sliced and sandwiched between sliced cherry tomatoes and fresh basil leaves, served with Sweet Balsamic Glaze

Crab Cakes 20

Crab cakes topped with buttered panko crumbs and baked in mini muffin tins, served with creamy Roasted Red Pepper Aioli

Seafood Cocktail Cups 26

Seafood salad with shrimp, bay scallops, sweet corn, red onion, cilantro, lime juice, chipotle cocktail sauce, tossed, scooped into small cucumber cups, and topped with crumbled queso fresco

Beef Empanadas 42

Buttery pastries filled with seasoned ground beef, herbs, spices, and green olives

Meat Loaves 59

All-beef meat loaves made in mini loaf pans, topped with a brown sugar-ginger glaze, and baked

Fudge Puppies 94

Mini waffles dunked in melted chocolate and rolled in crushed banana chips

Raspberry Champagne Cocktails 139

Sweetened raspberry puree mixed with raspberry vodka and finished with sparkling wine, served in shot glasses

One-Bite

"ONION" RINGS

serves 4 to 6

Beer-battered shallot rings are a fun, miniature take on one of America's favorite bar foods. The sweet, strong shallot and garlic flavors pair well with Buttermilk Ranch Sauce (page 22).

6 large shallots, sliced 1/4 inch thick
2 cups buttermilk
2 cups all-purpose flour, divided
2 teaspoons garlic powder
2 teaspoons smoked paprika
1 teaspoon salt
1/2 teaspoon freshly ground black pepper
2 cups beer*

2 quarts vegetable oil, for frying
About 3/4 cup Buttermilk Ranch Sauce, page 22

* *An American-style lager like PBR keeps the batter light and mild in flavor.*

1. Separate shallot slices into rings. Place in a large bowl and pour buttermilk over them. Refrigerate for about 2 hours. *{Tip: Soaking the shallots in buttermilk before battering and frying will help the flour mixture and batter adhere and form a light and crispy coating.}*
2. Preheat oil to 350°F. For the beer batter, place 1 cup of the flour, garlic powder, paprika, salt, and pepper in a shallow dish and stir together. Place the remaining 1 cup flour in a mixing bowl and whisk in beer until no lumps remain. Remove shallots from buttermilk and dredge them in the dry mixture and then the beer mixture, shaking off excess as you go.
3. Carefully drop the battered rings into the hot oil in small batches and fry for 4 to 6 minutes, or until golden brown and crispy. Drain rings on paper towels and season with salt. Serve immediately with ranch sauce.

Snack-Size

SEAFOOD COCKTAIL CUPS

makes 30

If you like shrimp cocktail and spicy flavors, you're bound to enjoy this fiery seafood snack served in refreshing cucumber cups. For a milder flavor, omit the chipotles and adobo sauce and add a little extra cocktail sauce.

SEAFOOD COCKTAIL

½ cup cocktail sauce
2 chipotle peppers in adobo,* minced
3 tablespoons adobo sauce
Juice of 1 lime
½ pound cooked tiger shrimp, peeled and chopped
¼ pound cooked bay scallops, quartered
½ cup frozen sweet corn, thawed
¼ medium red onion, diced (about 1/2 cup)
2 tablespoons thinly sliced chives
2 tablespoons minced cilantro

CUCUMBER CUPS

3 hothouse cucumbers, cut into 1-inch pieces
Salt and pepper, to taste

GARNISH

Crumbled queso fresco,** to taste

1. For the seafood cocktail, whisk together cocktail sauce, chipotles, adobo, and lime juice in a small bowl. In a large mixing bowl, combine shrimp, scallops, corn, onions, chives, and cilantro. Fold in sauce. Cover bowl and refrigerate.
2. For the cucumber cups, use a melon baller to gently scoop out half of the flesh from the inside of each piece of cucumber, creating a cup. Spoon 1 tablespoon of seafood cocktail into each cucumber cup. Top with a sprinkle of queso fresco and serve immediately, or chill until ready to serve.

Make any salad into finger food! A melon baller is the perfect tool for turning thick cucumber slices into little edible cups.

* *Cans of chipotle peppers in adobo are available in the Latin foods section of most supermarkets. You can substitute 1 to 2 tablespoons of hot sauce.*

** Queso fresco *means "fresh cheese," but it is also the name of a creamy, mild white cheese that crumbles easily. Mild feta is a good alternative.*

Li'l PAJEON

makes 24

Savory Korean pancakes called *pajeon* (pronounced *pa-jee-yeon*) are a popular appetizer. Their name comes from their main ingredients: *pa* means "green onion" and *jeon* means "pancake." If you don't fancy shrimp, you can always replace it with the seafood of your choice or omit it altogether for a vegetarian version of this tasty dish. Either way, these are delicious served with spicy Sesame-Soy Dipping Sauce.

- ½ cup all-purpose flour
- 2 tablespoons rice flour
- ½ cup ice water
- 3 tablespoons vegetable oil, divided
- 1 teaspoon salt
- 1 egg, lightly beaten
- 3 green onions, thinly sliced
- ½ pound tiger shrimp, finely chopped
- About ½ cup Sesame-Soy Dipping Sauce (page 30)

1. For the pancakes, combine flours, water, ½ tablespoon of the oil, salt, and egg in a mixing bowl and whisk together until smooth. Fold in green onions and shrimp until just combined.
2. Pour 1½ tablespoons of the oil into a large nonstick skillet and place over medium-high heat. Ladle 2-tablespoon rounds onto the hot surface, about 1 inch apart, and cook for 3 to 4 minutes on each side. Transfer to paper towels and repeat with the remaining oil and batter. Serve immediately with Sesame-Soy Dipping Sauce.

In Korean, "tiny food" is called ja-gun *(tiny)* ium-sheeg *(food).*

Homemade Condiments

SESAME-SOY DIPPING SAUCE

makes about 1/2 cup

Serve this tasty sauce alongside Li'l Pajeon and other dunkable Asian snacks, like tempura vegetables and fried or steamed dumplings.

1. In a small bowl, whisk all ingredients together to combine.

- 1/3 cup soy sauce
- 3 tablespoons sesame oil
- 1 1/2 tablespoons Korean hot chili powder (*gochugaru*)
- 2 teaspoons toasted sesame seeds
- 1/2 teaspoon sugar
- 1 garlic clove, minced
- 1 green onion, thinly sliced

Gochugaru *is a staple in Korean cooking. It's a spicy red chili powder that can be found in most Asian supermarkets and some gourmet grocery stores. If you can't find it, cayenne pepper is a good substitute.*

CUCUMBER-MINT RAITA

makes about 2 cups

Raita (pronounced *RYE-tah* or *ROY-taw*) is a cool cucumber-mint yogurt dipping sauce you won't want to live without. This Indian staple can be made with spinach instead of fresh mint.

1. In a small bowl, whisk together all ingredients until well combined. Cover and refrigerate.

- 1 cucumber, peeled, seeded, and grated
- 1 cup Greek yogurt
- Juice of 1 lemon
- 1 tablespoon minced fresh mint
- 1 teaspoon salt
- 1/2 teaspoon paprika
- 1/2 teaspoon ground cumin

A Little Menu

→ TINY VEGETARIAN FOOD PARTY ←

If you (or your guests) don't eat meat, you can still put out a hearty little spread! Here's a collection of some of our favorite vegetarian recipes.

Caprese Skewers 10

Small mozzarella balls sliced and sandwiched between sliced cherry tomatoes and fresh basil leaves, served with Sweet Balsamic Glaze

"Onion" Rings 25

Shallots thinly sliced, battered, fried, and served with Creamy Buttermilk Ranch Sauce

Potato Samosas 32

Spiced potato and vegetable filling stuffed into pieces of dough and baked or fried and served with raita, a cucumber yogurt sauce

Sweet Potato Latkes 48

Shredded sweet potato and green onion latkes served with sour cream

Mac 'n' Cheese Bites 85

Creamy mac 'n' cheese cut into small triangles, coated in panko bread crumbs, and deep-fried

Éclairs 114

Homemade éclairs (pâte à choux) filled with vanilla pastry cream, with the tops dipped in melted chocolate

Pineapple Upside-Down Cakes 140

Sweet whiskey, triple sec, vanilla vodka, and pineapple juice cocktail shots

Small

POTATO SAMOSAS

makes 48

This classic Indian snack food is served with *raita*, a traditional cucumber-mint yogurt sauce, to cool the palate and offset the spicy notes of the samosa filling. Set out big bowls of samosas and fresh cucumber-mint raita, and get to dipping!

2 russet potatoes, peeled and diced
1 tablespoon extra-virgin olive oil
$\frac{1}{4}$ medium yellow onion, diced (about $\frac{1}{2}$ cup)
2 garlic cloves, minced
2 teaspoons ground cumin
1 teaspoon garam masala*
1 teaspoon ground coriander
$\frac{1}{2}$ teaspoon ground cinnamon
$\frac{2}{3}$ cup frozen petite peas, thawed
1 (16-ounce) can store-bought biscuit dough, cut into 24 equal pieces
Salt and pepper, to taste

2 cups Cucumber-Mint Raita (page 30)

**Garam masala, a lovely blend of aromatic spices used in Indian cuisine, can be purchased in most grocery stores and in specialty Indian markets.*

1. Preheat oven to 375°F.
2. Place potatoes in a large pot, cover with water, and bring to a boil. Boil for 15 to 20 minutes, or until potatoes are fork-tender. Drain and transfer potatoes to a large mixing bowl.
3. Warm oil in a skillet over medium-high heat. Sauté onions and garlic for about 4 minutes, then add them to potatoes. Add cumin, garam masala, coriander, and cinnamon and stir until well combined. Fold in peas and season with salt and pepper.
4. Take 1 piece of dough and, in the palm of your hand, form a small thin round, $3\frac{1}{2}$ to 4 inches in diameter. Roll it into a wide cone and stuff with a heaping tablespoon of filling. Seal edges with the back of a fork to create a triangle. Repeat with remaining pieces of dough and filling. Place samosas on a baking sheet lined with parchment paper and bake for 20 to 25 minutes, or until golden brown. Serve warm with raita.

For a delicious variation, try replacing the potatoes with steamed and diced cauliflower. Other popular samosa ingredients include chicken, beef, lamb, or vegetables.

Baby

BOLINHOS DE BACALHAU

makes 40

This popular Portuguese snack (pronounced *boll-in-yoos de ba-cal-yao*) is a flavorful version of cod fritters. We've kicked things up a notch by pairing our mini appetizer with a zesty lemon-caper dipping sauce. It's like fish sticks and tartar sauce for grown-ups!

1 lemon, halved
2 sprigs fresh thyme
1 pound salted cod fillets,* soaked overnight in cold water (replace water every few hours) and drained
1 cup mashed potatoes, warmed
1 tablespoon extra-virgin olive oil
¼ medium sweet onion, peeled and diced (about ½ cup)
3 garlic cloves, minced
4 green onions, thinly sliced
1 egg, lightly beaten
3 tablespoons minced fresh flat-leaf parsley
Salt and pepper, to taste
1 quart vegetable oil for frying
About ½ cup Lemon-Caper Dipping Sauce (page 36)

** Salted cod fillets can be difficult to find; a fair substitute is poaching the cod fillets in a mixture of 3 cups clam juice and ½ cup salt. For an extra-briny flavor, add diced olives to the shredded fish mix.*

1. Fill a medium pot three-fourths with water. Squeeze in lemon juice and drop in lemon halves. Add thyme. Over medium heat, bring liquid to a simmer. Add drained cod fillets and poach for 15 minutes. Discard poaching liquid.
2. In a large mixing bowl, shred fillets with two forks (or use your fingers). Add mashed potatoes and mix until just combined.
3. Warm oil in a medium skillet over medium-high heat. Add onions and garlic and sauté until translucent, 3 to 5 minutes. Add to fish mixture along with green onions, egg, parsley, and salt and pepper. Gently fold to combine. Form mixture into small balls, about 2 tablespoons each, and place on a baking sheet lined with parchment paper. Refrigerate for 30 minutes to 1 hour. *{Tip: Refrigerating helps firm up the fish balls so they won't fall apart when fried.}*
4. In a large pot, preheat oil to 365°F. Fry fish balls in small batches for 4 to 6 minutes, or until golden brown. Drain on paper towels and season with pepper. Serve immediately with Lemon-Caper Dipping Sauce.

Because they pair so well with cold beer, crunchy hot bolinhos de bacalhau are a popular appetizer in Portuguese and Brazilian bars.

Homemade Condiments

LEMON-CAPER DIPPING SAUCE

makes about 1/2 cup

This zesty, creamy sauce is delightful as a dip or a topping for chicken, lamb, and fish dishes (like Bolinhos de Bacalhau, page 35).

1/3 cup mayonnaise (regular or light)
2 tablespoons sour cream (regular or light)
3 tablespoons minced capers
Zest and juice of 1 lemon
1 garlic clove, minced
1/2 teaspoon dry mustard
1/4 teaspoon cayenne pepper
Salt and pepper, to taste

1. In a medium bowl, stir to combine mayonnaise, sour cream, capers, lemon zest and juice, garlic, dry mustard, and cayenne pepper. Season with salt and pepper. Use immediately or cover and refrigerate.

AVOCADO CILANTRO SAUCE

makes about 1 cup

Avocado lovers, rejoice! This versatile sauce is the perfect companion for spicy Latin dishes like the Tiny Taquitos on page 38. Make it ahead so the flavors have time to meld.

2/3 cup sour cream
1/2 avocado, peeled and pitted
1/2 bunch cilantro, roughly chopped
Juice of 1 lime
Salt and pepper, to taste

1. In the bowl of a food processor, combine sour cream, avocado, cilantro, and lime juice. Process until smooth, about 1 minute. Season with salt and pepper; pulse to combine. Use immediately or cover and refrigerate.

A Little Menu

TINY COMFORT FOOD PARTY

If the weather outside is cold and dreary or you just need a little heartwarming snack or pick-me-up, here's one of our favorite menus for cozy comfort foods. Guaranteed to chase the winter blues away.

Coxhina 41

Shredded chicken, cream cheese, sweet corn, and green onions wrapped in dough and fried crispy hot

Shepherd's Pies 56

Puff pastry cups filled with a mix of seasoned ground lamb or beef, sautéed carrots, corn, and peas and topped with Creamy Mashed Potatoes

Meat Loaves 59

All-beef meat loaves made in mini loaf pans, topped with a brown sugar-ginger glaze, and baked

Deep-Dish Pizzas 60

Biscuit dough formed in mini muffin tins and filled with Italian sausage, diced bell peppers, and mozzarella, topped with tomato sauce and grated Parmesan

Chicken 'n' Waffles 70

Buttered mini waffles topped with small pieces of buttermilk-fried chicken tenders and a drizzle of sweet maple syrup

White Chocolate Cheesecakes 99

Cheesecakes baked in mini muffin tins and drizzled with sweet and tangy blueberry compote

Bloody Marys 136

Soju (Korean rice wine) bloody marys with Sriracha, served in shot glasses with pickled green beans and a fried quail's egg

Tiny TAQUITOS

makes 24

These little crunchy and savory delights are like two-bite tacos—perfect party fare. Creamy Avocado Cilantro Sauce offers a cooling counterpoint to the spicy shredded chicken filling.

2 quarts vegetable oil, for frying

CHICKEN FILLING

1½ cups finely shredded cooked chicken

½ cup prepared salsa

2 tablespoons adobo sauce

1 tablespoon ancho chili powder

1 teaspoon cayenne pepper

Salt and pepper, to taste

1½ tablespoons honey

24 small (2- to 3-inch) corn tortillas*

About ½ cup Avocado Cilantro Sauce, page 36

** Mini corn tortillas are available at Mexican supermarkets and gourmet grocery stores. If you can't find them, use a 2- or 3-inch circle cutter to trim small tortillas out of larger ones.*

1. In a large pot, preheat oil to 350°F.
2. In a large mixing bowl, toss to combine chicken, salsa, adobo, chili powder, and cayenne pepper. Season with salt and pepper. Drizzle honey over mixture and gently fold to incorporate.
3. Place about 1½ tablespoons of filling onto each tortilla and carefully roll into a long, thin tube. Secure the rolled taquitos with toothpicks.
4. In small batches, fry taquitos for 4 to 6 minutes, or until crisp and lightly golden brown. Drain on paper towels and remove toothpicks. Serve immediately, with sauce for dipping.

COXINHA

makes 20

This fun Brazilian street food is traditionally formed into the shape of a drumstick to represent the main filling ingredient: chicken. In fact, *coxinha* (pronounced co-*SHEEN-ya*) means "little chicken drumsticks" in Portuguese. We like to make them extra mini for snacking.

1 quart vegetable oil, for frying
3½ cups low-sodium chicken broth
1 onion, peeled and quartered
1 carrot, peeled and quartered
1 celery rib, quartered

CHICKEN FILLING
1 large chicken breast
8 ounces packaged cream cheese, softened
1 ear corn, kernels cut off the cob
2 green onions, thinly sliced
1 garlic clove, minced
Salt and pepper, to taste

½ tablespoon extra-virgin olive oil
2 cups all-purpose flour
1 egg
1 tablespoon whole milk
1 cup plain Italian bread crumbs
Salt and pepper, to taste

1. In a large pot, preheat oil to 350°F. In another large pot, combine broth, onions, carrots, and celery and bring to a simmer. Carefully add chicken, cover, and reduce heat to medium-low. Poach chicken for 12 to 15 minutes, or until just cooked through. Turn off heat, but leave the pot of hot poaching liquid on the stove. Remove chicken from liquid and let it rest for 10 minutes.
2. For the filling, finely chop or shred chicken into a large mixing bowl. Add cream cheese, corn, green onions, and garlic. Season with salt and pepper. Fold to combine.
3. Strain 1½ cups of the poaching liquid and discard the rest. In a saucepan over high heat, bring reserved liquid and oil to a boil. Add flour and stir vigorously until dough forms. Turn dough out onto a lightly floured surface and knead until smooth, about 5 minutes. Roll out to ¼ inch thick. Cut out small rounds using a 3-inch circle cutter or the rim of a round cup. Place a small scoop (about 1 tablespoon) of the filling in the center of each round. Pinch dough together at the top to seal, creating plump little teardrop-shaped pouches. In a small bowl, lightly whisk eggs and milk together. Place bread crumbs in another small bowl. Carefully dip each pouch into the egg wash and then the bread crumbs until fully coated. Fry coxinha in small batches for 7 to 9 minutes, or until golden brown. Drain on paper towels, lightly season with salt, and serve hot.

Coxinha freeze well and can be made at least a week ahead. There's no need to thaw before frying.

Snack-Size

BEEF EMPANADAS

makes 24

It's hard not to love these bite-size meat-stuffed pastries from Spain. They're filled with ground beef, lots of flavorful smoky spices, diced boiled egg, and briny green olives for extra kick. The buttery crust and fun crescent shape make these snack-size empanadas a perfect appetizer.

FILLING

3½ tablespoons extra-virgin olive oil, divided
½ pound ground beef
¼ medium yellow onion, diced (about ½ cup)
3 garlic cloves, minced
2 teaspoons smoked paprika
2 teaspoons ground cumin
1 teaspoon curry powder
¼ teaspoon ground cinnamon
¼ cup pitted and diced green olives
1 hard-boiled egg, peeled and diced
Salt and pepper, to taste

WRAPPING

1 package store-bought pie dough, or homemade (page 126)
1 egg

1. Preheat oven to 400°F. Line a baking sheet with parchment paper or silicone baking mats.
2. In a skillet over medium-high heat, warm 2 tablespoons of the oil. Add beef and brown for about 5 minutes, stirring occasionally. Season with salt and pepper. Transfer beef to a medium mixing bowl, draining off excess liquid.
3. Add the remaining 1½ tablespoons oil to pan and return to heat. Add onions and garlic and sauté for 5 minutes. Return beef to pan (don't wash the bowl). Add paprika, cumin, curry powder, and cinnamon. Sauté for 1 more minute. Pour mixture back into mixing bowl, gently fold in olives and eggs, and season with salt and pepper. Let cool slightly.
4. Place pie dough on a lightly floured surface and cut out 24 rounds with a 3- or 4-inch circle cutter or the rim of a round cup. In a small bowl, whisk together egg and 1 tablespoon water. Place 1 tablespoon of filling in the center of each round. Brush edges with egg wash. Press edges together to create a semicircle and seal with the back of a fork. Brush the tops with egg wash and make 2 small incisions for ventilation. Place on prepared baking sheet and bake for 15 to 20 minutes, or until golden brown. Serve warm.

You can simply crimp the edges with a fork or create a decorative edge: Starting at one end, fold the edge over at a slight angle and press to seal. Repeat until completely sealed.

Delicious
EMPANADA FILLINGS

Mini empanadas are endlessly versatile. You can stuff these pastries with almost anything to suit your fancy, whether savory or sweet. Here are a few of our favorite flavor combinations.

VEGETARIAN EMPANADAS: Replace the beef with 8 ounces soy chorizo and combine with the remaining filling ingredients.

SEAFOOD EMPANADAS: Toss ½ pound cooked and diced tiger shrimp with 1 teaspoon cumin, 1 teaspoon smoked paprika, 1 tablespoon minced capers, 1 diced hard-boiled egg, and 1 tablespoon extra-virgin olive oil.

DESSERT EMPANADAS: Fill each pastry with 1 tablespoon dulce de leche or caramel, 1 mini marshmallow, ½ teaspoon toasted and minced hazelnuts, and a pinch of cinnamon. Fill and form empanadas and bake as above.

A Little Menu

TINY FOOD FIESTA

What's more fun than a tiny Latin food fiesta? We love to serve big platters of a selection of tiny foods alongside tasty sweets and refreshing fizzes to cool the heat.

Taquitos 38

Three-inch corn tortillas filled with seasoned shredded chicken, rolled, fried, and served with avocado and cilantro sauce

Beef Empanadas 42

Buttery pastries filled with seasoned ground beef, herbs, spices, and green olives

Arepas 53

Small round cornmeal cakes stuffed with seasoned spicy chicken and shredded iceberg, with a drizzle of creamy avocado sauce

Fried Tacos 82

Three-inch corn tortillas filled with shredded chicken and fried, then finished with iceberg, queso fresco, and a dash of hot sauce

Candied Bacon Churros 113

Caramelized bacon mixed into churro batter, fried, and tossed in a light coating of cinnamon-sugar

Sweet Corn Ice Cream Tacos 129

Homemade ice cream served in tiny fried corn tortilla shells and topped with "candied corn"

Lemon-Lime Fizzes 150

Light beer, citrus vodka, lemonade concentrate, lemon-lime soda, and fresh lime zest served in shot glasses

Pint-Size

JALAPEÑO CHEDDAR CORN STICKS

makes 40

These little corn cakes are packed with spicy jalapeños and cheddar-cheesy goodness. We often bake them in mini corn stick tins (like the one on page 154) so they're shaped like cobs. Whether you bake them in mini corn stick tins or mini muffin tins, you'll have mini jalapeño cheddar corn goodness!

- 2/3 cup yellow cornmeal
- 1/4 cup all-purpose flour
- 3/4 teaspoon baking powder
- 1/2 teaspoon granulated sugar
- 1/8 teaspoon baking soda
- 1/4 teaspoon salt
- 1 egg, lightly beaten
- 1/2 cup whole milk
- 1/4 cup plus 1 tablespoon honey, plus extra for drizzling
- 2 tablespoons unsalted butter, melted
- 2 large jalapeños, seeded and diced
- 1/2 cup grated mild cheddar cheese

1. Preheat oven to 375°F. Coat the inside of a mini corn stick pan or a mini muffin tin with cooking spray.
2. In a large bowl, combine cornmeal, flour, baking powder, sugar, baking soda, and salt. In another large bowl, whisk together egg, milk, honey, and butter. Add the dry mixture to the wet mixture, stirring until well combined and no lumps remain. Gently fold jalapeños and cheese into the batter. Fill each mini corn or muffin mold about two-thirds full.
3. Bake for 7 to 9 minutes if using a mini corn stick tin or 20 to 25 minutes if using a mini muffin tin, until golden brown. Pop corn cakes out of pan and drizzle with extra honey. Serve warm.

Bring these bite-size delights to any picnic or cookout. They're great buttered up and dipped into a bowl of hearty chili. Or just pop a few morsels in your mouth for a satisfying afternoon snack.

Little SWEET POTATO LATKES

makes 30

Traditionally served on Hanukah, these low-maintenance potato pancakes are tasty and filling. We jazzed up the classic recipe by swapping out the typical white spuds for bright orange sweet potatoes and adding flavorful green onions.

1. Place sweet potato between 2 sheets of cheesecloth; grasp ends of cheesecloth and twist to extract as much liquid as possible. *{Tip: The more liquid you squeeze out of the potato, the better the latkes will hold together while frying.}*
2. In a large mixing bowl, toss drained sweet potato with green onions, shallots, and garlic. Sprinkle flour over the mixture and fold to combine. Stir in egg until fully incorporated. Season with salt and pepper.
3. Warm oil in a cast-iron skillet over medium-high heat. Drop dollops of batter, about 2 tablespoons each, into the hot skillet and fry on each side for about 4 to 5 minutes, or until golden brown. Drain latkes on paper towels and season with salt and pepper. Top each latke with a small dollop of crème fraîche or serve it on the side as a dipping sauce. Serve warm.

LATKES

1 sweet potato, peeled and coarsely grated (about 1½ cups)
3 green onions, thinly sliced
1 shallot, minced
1 garlic clove, minced
3½ tablespoons all-purpose flour
1 egg, lightly beaten
Salt and pepper, to taste
¼ cup vegetable oil

GARNISH

⅔ cup crème fraîche*

** Crème fraîche is available at many supermarkets and gourmet grocery stores. Sour cream or Greek yogurt make good substitutes.*

Chapter 2

TINY DINNER PARTY!

Itty-Bitty Entrees

Addictive
AREPAS

makes 24

These savory stuffed corn cakes are so versatile, you can enjoy them anytime and fill them with your choice of flavors. *Arepas* (*ah-RAY-pas*) are a classic Venezuelan snack that can be eaten with nothing but a pat of butter or cut in half, filled with shredded chicken, and topped with a creamy avocado sauce called *guasacaca* (*WAH-sa-ca-ca*).

1. In a mixing bowl, stir together cornmeal, hot water, oil, and salt until mixture just comes together. Cover with a damp towel and let rest for at least 15 to 20 minutes. *{Tip: The longer the dough sits before it's formed, the better it can fully absorb the liquid.}*
2. Mix dough with your hands to remove any lumps. Take about 3 tablespoons of dough and form a flat, thin disk. Lightly brush both sides with vegetable oil and place on a sheet pan lined with parchment paper.
3. Warm a little vegetable oil in a heavy-bottomed skillet over medium-high heat. Once skillet is hot, add a few arepas, making sure not to overcrowd them, and cook for 6 to 8 minutes on each side, until they are golden brown and make a hollow sound when tapped. *{Tip: If the arepas begin to smoke, lower heat to medium and continue to cook.}* Transfer cooked arepas to a parchment-paper-lined sheet pan and keep in a warm oven while you cook the remaining dough.
4. Use a paring knife to open each arepa like a pocket. Fill with chicken and top with a generous drizzle of guasacaca and a sprinkle of queso fresco.

DOUGH

1 cup harina pan* (precooked cornmeal)
1¼ cups hot water
1½ tablespoons vegetable oil, plus more for brushing and cooking
½ teaspoon salt

1½ cups shredded cooked chicken
1 cup Guasacaca (page 54)
¼ cup crumbled queso fresco**

** Harina pan (often labeled Harina PAN) can be found at Latin grocery stores.*

*** Queso fresco is a fresh cow's milk cheese that is crumbly. Find it at grocery stores and Latin markets. Any mild feta cheese is a fine substitute.*

Mix the dough and prepare your favorite fillings ahead, and then have friends over to assemble and eat lots of little arepas!

Homemade Condiments

CREAMY AVOCADO GUASACACA

makes about 1 cup

Guasacaca is much like guacamole, but it has a lovely vinegary tang and is never mashed; all the ingredients are roughly hand-chopped, then pureed until smooth. Serve it fresh with grilled meats, chicken, and arepas like the ones on page 53.

- ½ avocado, peeled, pitted, and quartered
- ¼ small sweet onion, peeled and quartered
- 1 garlic clove, chopped
- 1 Serrano pepper, halved and seeded
- 1½ tablespoons white wine vinegar
- Juice of ½ lime
- ½ bunch cilantro, stemmed
- 1½ tablespoons vegetable oil
- Salt and pepper, to taste

1. Place avocado, onion, garlic, serrano chili, vinegar, and lime juice in a blender. Process until smooth.
2. Add cilantro, oil, and salt, and blend until smooth. Season to taste with more salt and pepper. Serve immediately or cover and refrigerate.

A Tiny Food Party Trick

⟶ CREAMY MASHED POTATOES ⟵

makes about 1 1/2 cups

This recipe makes smooth and creamy mashed potatoes, ideal for piping pretty little clouds onto bite-size appetizers like the Baby-Size Shepherd's Pies on page 56.

1 russet potato, peeled and cut into 2-inch chunks
1/4 cup (1/2 stick) unsalted butter, softened
1/4 cup heavy cream
1 garlic clove, minced

1. Place potato chunks in a large pot and fill with water to cover. Bring to a boil and continue boiling until the potatoes are fork-tender, 15 to 20 minutes. Place butter, cream, and garlic in a small saucepan over medium-low heat and bring to a simmer. Remove from heat and cover to keep hot.
2. Drain potatoes and return them to their pot. Mash and gradually add the heated cream mixture, until potatoes are smooth and creamy. Season with salt and pepper. *{Tip: Scoop mashed potatoes into a piping bag fitted with a star tip to pipe swirls of fluffy mashed potatoes onto hors d'oeuvres.}* Use immediately or cover and refrigerate.

PIPING TIPS AND TRICKS: *To pipe perfect swirls and puffs, use a pastry bag fitted with a round tip or star tip (like the ones on page 154) and twist the open end for even pressure. If you don't have a piping bag, simply load mashed potatoes (or other fillings and toppings) into a zip-top plastic bag. Snip off about 1/4 inch of one corner and pipe away!*

Baby-Size
SHEPHERD'S PIES

makes 24

This cozy cottage fare is so hearty that it's perfect served in petite portions. Fluffy mashed potatoes top a savory meat-and-veggie filling served in flaky mini piecrusts.

PIES

2 sheets store-bought frozen puff pastry, thawed

About 1½ cups mashed potatoes, store-bought or homemade (page 55)

SAVORY FILLING

3 tablespoons extra-virgin olive oil, divided

½ pound ground lamb or ground beef

2 tablespoons minced tarragon

2 tablespoons thinly sliced chives

1 tablespoon cumin

½ tablespoon garlic powder

Salt and pepper, to taste

1 shallot, diced

1 carrot, peeled and diced

1 ear of corn, kernels removed from cob (about ½ cup)

½ cup frozen peas, thawed

1. Preheat oven to 425°F. Using a 2-inch circle cutter, punch 24 rounds out of puff pastry. Coat a mini muffin tin with nonstick cooking spray and gently press the rounds into the molds. Prick the bottoms of the puff pastry cups with a fork to prevent them from rising. Freeze until ready to use. Prepare mashed potatoes.
2. Warm 1 tablespoon of the oil in a skillet over medium-high heat, add lamb, and let it cook until browned, about 3 minutes. Stir in tarragon, chives, cumin, and garlic powder. Season with salt and pepper and remove from heat. Pour mixture into a medium bowl. Place skillet back over heat and add remaining oil. Sauté shallots and carrots for 2 minutes. Add corn and continue to sauté for 5 minutes. Return meat mixture to pan and stir together. Fold in peas. Season with salt and pepper.
3. Scoop a small amount of the filling into each puff pastry cup. Bake for 20 to 25 minutes, or until pastry shells are golden brown. Let cool slightly before removing pies from muffin tins. Scoop mashed potatoes into a piping bag fitted with a star tip and pipe a dollop onto the top of each. Season with pepper and serve.

You can speed up this recipe by using leftover or store-bought mashed potatoes; simply reheat them before piping them onto the pies.

Miniature

MEAT LOAVES

makes 8

Remember Mom's meat loaf? This is our grown-up—and bite-size—take on the classic comfort food.

1. Preheat oven to 375°F. Place onions, carrots, garlic, beef, pork, oats, and egg in a bowl and mix together until well combined. Season with salt and pepper. Gently fold in oregano, thyme, and rosemary. Shape the meat mixture into eight 2-ounce loaves (about 1/4 cup each). Place in a lightly greased mini loaf pan and repeat with remaining meat mixture.

2. In a small bowl, whisk together glaze ingredients. Set aside half of the mixture. Brush tops of the meat loaves with half of the glaze and bake for 30 minutes. Remove pan from oven and drain accumulated liquid. Brush tops of loaves with the remaining glaze and bake for an additional 10 minutes. Remove meat loaves from pan and let cool for 7 minutes before slicing. Serve warm.

No need for silverware! To serve, cut these mini meat loaves into thin (1/4- to 1/2-inch) slices and skewer with cocktail picks (pictured, page 58) or cocktail forks (see Supplies, page 155). Your guests can pick up and eat bite-size meat-loaf pops.

MEAT LOAF

1/2 small yellow onion, diced
1 carrot, peeled and diced
2 garlic cloves, minced
1/2 pound lean ground beef
1/2 pound ground pork
1/2 cup instant oats*
1 egg, lightly beaten
Salt and pepper, to taste
1 1/2 tablespoons minced oregano
1 tablespoon minced thyme
1/2 tablespoon minced rosemary

GLAZE

3/4 cup ketchup
3 tablespoons light brown sugar, packed
1 tablespoon honey
2 teaspoons ground ginger

** If you prefer meat loaf with a smoother texture, finely grind instant oats in a food processor before adding them to the meat mixture.*

Super-Small

DEEP-DISH PIZZAS

makes 24

We've shrunk this Chicago favorite to miniature proportions but still managed to cram in all the delicious, familiar flavors: Italian sausage, bell peppers, and gooey mozzarella.

1 (14.5-ounce) can diced tomatoes
1/2 cup red wine
1 tablespoon minced oregano
2 garlic cloves, minced
Salt and pepper, to taste
1 (16-ounce) can store-bought biscuit dough
1/2 pound Italian sausage, casings removed
1 green bell pepper, seeded and diced
1 1/2 cups shredded mozzarella
1/4 cup grated Parmesan cheese

1. Preheat oven to 400°F. Place tomatoes, wine, oregano, and garlic in a small saucepan over medium heat; season with salt and pepper. Simmer for 30 minutes, stirring occasionally. Set aside and let cool.
2. Cut each piece of biscuit dough into thirds. Lightly grease 24 small (2-inch) tart shell tins and place a piece in the center of each. Gently press and spread dough along the bottom and up the sides of the tin. *{Tip: If you don't have small tart shell tins, use a muffin tin.}*
3. Press 1 tablespoon of the sausage into each piece of dough and top with a sprinkle of peppers. Toss mozzarella and half of the Parmesan in a small bowl and sprinkle mixture over top. Spoon 1 tablespoon of sauce over the cheeses and sprinkle with the remaining Parmesan.
4. Bake for 25 to 30 minutes, or until cheese begins to bubble and crusts are golden brown. Let pizzas cool for a few minutes before removing from pans. Serve warm.

Pizza party! Other awesome toppings for these deep-dish bites are chopped mushrooms, pepperoni, olives, and even diced Canadian ham and pineapple.

Baby BBQ PULLED PORK SANDWICHES

makes 12

In addition to savory pulled pork and tangy homemade sauce, our version of this popular barbecue fare includes the crunchy, salty goodness of peanuts.

PULLED PORK

1 2-pound pork butt or shoulder*
2 cups low-sodium chicken broth
1 cup root beer
1 yellow onion, chopped
2 bay leaves
1 teaspoon mustard seeds, lightly crushed

FIXINS

½ cup chopped dry-roasted peanuts
About 2 cups barbeque sauce, store-bought or homemade (page 64)
12 Hawaiian rolls, sliced in half
About 1 cup coleslaw, store-bought or homemade (page 64)

** Or 3 cups cooked pulled pork.*

1. Put pork, broth, root beer, onion, bay leaves, and mustard seeds in a slow cooker on low heat for about 6 hours or until the pork is tender.
2. Remove meat and discard liquid. Using 2 forks or your hands, shred the meat. Return shredded meat to the slow cooker and keep on low heat for 10 minutes or until you're ready to serve.
3. Toss pork, peanuts, and barbecue sauce together in a large bowl until thoroughly combined. Fill each roll with about ¼ cup pulled pork and 2 heaping tablespoons of slaw.

For a mini Southern feast, serve with mini Cokes, Tiny Potato Salad Bites (page 19), and a side of One-Bite "Onion" Rings (page 25).

Homemade Toppings

CREAMY TANGY SLAW

makes about 1 cup

Homemade coleslaw is a tasty side and a delicious topping for sandwiches like Baby BBQ Pulled Pork Sandwiches.

- 1/2 cup shredded green cabbage
- 1/4 cup shredded purple cabbage
- 1 medium carrot, peeled and grated
- 1/3 cup mayonnaise (regular or light)
- 2 1/2 tablespoons apple cider vinegar
- Juice of 1/2 lemon
- Salt and pepper, to taste

1. In a medium bowl, toss to combine cabbage and carrots. In a small bowl, whisk together mayonnaise, vinegar, and lemon juice. Season with salt and pepper.
2. Pour dressing over vegetables and toss until well coated. Let slaw sit for about 30 minutes before serving.

BARBECUE SAUCE

makes 2 cups

This tasty sauce can be made up to 5 days in advance and stored in the refrigerator. It's perfect for dipping Mini Corn Dogs (page 69) or topping Baby BBQ Pulled Pork Sandwiches (page 63).

- 3 strips bacon, roughly chopped
- 2 tablespoons extra-virgin olive oil
- 3 shallots, diced
- 3 garlic cloves, minced
- Salt and pepper, to taste
- 3 tablespoons minced fresh thyme
- 2 tablespoons thinly sliced chives
- 3 cups ketchup
- 1/3 cup light brown sugar, packed
- 1/3 cup molasses
- 3 tablespoons apple cider vinegar
- 1 1/2 tablespoons dry mustard
- 1 tablespoon ground cumin
- 2 teaspoons ground ginger
- 2 teaspoons chili powder
- 1/4 teaspoon ground cinnamon

1. In a medium saucepan, sauté bacon over medium-high heat until crispy and browned, about 5 minutes. Remove bacon with a slotted spoon and drain all but 2 tablespoons of the fat from the pan. Add olive oil to pan and place back over medium-high heat. Add shallots and garlic and sauté for 3 to 4 minutes. Season with salt and pepper. Stir in thyme and chives and sauté for an additional 2 minutes. Add the cooked bacon back into the pan, followed by the remaining sauce ingredients and stir until fully combined.
2. Reduce heat to medium-low and simmer for 30 to 40 minutes, stirring occasionally. Pour sauce into a blender and puree until smooth. Serve immediately or cover and refrigerate.

A Little Menu

↦ TINY FOOD POTLUCK PLANNER ↤

Here's a collection of tasty recipes that are sure to steal the show at any potluck. Or give each friend a recipe, and then get together for a tiny potluck feast!

Caprese Skewers 10

Small mozzarella balls sliced and sandwiched between sliced cherry tomatoes and fresh basil leaves, served with Sweet Balsamic Glaze

Crab Cakes 20

Crab cakes topped with buttered panko crumbs and baked in mini muffin tins, served with creamy Roasted Red Pepper Aioli

Pajeon 29

Mini Korean-style seafood and vegetable pancakes served with Spicy Sesame Soy Sauce

Lamb Sliders 66

Juicy lamb burgers on mini sesame buns, filled with Roasted Red Pepper Aioli, caramelized onions, and Vermont white cheddar

Bánh Mì Sandwiches 81

Marinated and grilled pork belly, homemade pickled carrots and daikon matchsticks, cilantro, sliced Serrano peppers, sliced snacking cucumbers, and pâté all stuffed into mini baguettes

Chocolate Raspberry Tarts 100

Baked mini pie shells filled with chocolate ganache, topped with gold-dusted fresh raspberries

Orange Creamsicles 143

Vanilla vodka, triple sec, vanilla ice cream, and orange soda, mixed and garnished with an orange zest-and-sugar rim

Little LAMB SLIDERS

makes 16

For this ultimate burger made mini, we start with lamb rather than beef and combine it with tarragon and cumin. We top the juicy grilled patties with caramelized red onions and sandwich them between toasted slider rolls with fresh-made Roasted Red Pepper Aioli, sharp white cheddar, and baby arugula. Lamb sliders make an elegant, delectable addition to any party or get-together.

1. Line a baking sheet with parchment paper.
2. In a large mixing bowl, mix lamb, tarragon, cumin, and garlic just to combine; don't overwork the mixture. Season with salt and pepper. Pinch off 1-ounce handfuls (about 2 tablespoons each) and form into small patties. Place patties on the prepared sheet and refrigerate until ready to grill. *{Tip: Form the patties and make the aioli a day ahead to save time on party day.}*
3. Melt butter in a heavy-bottom skillet over medium-low heat for 3 to 4 minutes. Add onions. Sprinkle 2 tablespoons water and sugar overtop and reduce heat to low. Stir. Continue to cook over low heat, stirring frequently, for 30 to 40 minutes, until onions have wilted completely and are sweetened.
4. Preheat broiler. In a large grill pan, heat oil over medium heat. Add patties and cook for 5 to 7 minute on each side, depending on desired doneness. Transfer cooked patties to a sheet pan and top each with a square of cheese. Broil until cheese begins to bubble, about 2 minutes.
5. Spread aioli onto buns and top with a few arugula leaves, a lamb patty, and 1½ tablespoons of onions. Close buns and serve warm.

PATTIES

1 pound ground lamb
2 tablespoons minced tarragon
2 teaspoons ground cumin
1 garlic clove, minced
Salt and pepper, to taste
3 tablespoons extra-virgin olive oil

CARAMELIZED RED ONIONS

¼ cup (½ stick) unsalted butter
1 medium red onion, thinly sliced (about 2 cups)
½ teaspoon granulated sugar

TO FINISH

8 ounces sharp white cheddar cheese, sliced into ½-ounce (1½-inch) squares
About ¾ cup Roasted Red Pepper Aioli (page 22)
1 cup baby arugula
16 sesame slider rolls, split and toasted

Mini

CORN DOGS

makes 24

These are no ordinary corn dogs. The fragrant buttermilk-cornmeal batter is laced with a hint of honey, spices, and delicious crumbles of bacon.

1 quart vegetable oil, for frying
24 toothpicks or cocktail sticks

CORN DOGS

½ cup yellow cornmeal
¼ cup all-purpose flour
1 tablespoon sugar
1½ teaspoons cayenne pepper
1 teaspoon chili powder
½ teaspoon salt
½ teaspoon white pepper
½ teaspoon baking powder
⅛ teaspoon baking soda
⅓ cup buttermilk
1 egg
1 tablespoon honey
1 cup crumbled cooked bacon (about 9 strips)
24 cocktail wieners (such as Lit'l Smokies), or 6 hot dogs cut into 4 pieces each

1. In a medium pot, preheat oil to 365°F.
2. In a mixing bowl, stir together cornmeal, flour, sugar, cayenne pepper, chili powder, salt, white pepper, baking powder, and baking soda. *{Tip: If you prefer a smoother batter, pulse the cornmeal and flour together in a food processor before stirring in the remaining dry ingredients.}* Stir in buttermilk, egg, and honey and gently whisk until no lumps remain. Fold in bacon.
3. Skewer 1 cocktail wiener on each toothpick. Working in small batches, dip and roll wieners in batter until fully coated and then quickly and carefully drop them, toothpick and all, into the hot oil. Fry for 3 to 4 minutes, until golden brown. Drain on paper towels.

Serve trays of warm corn dogs with a side of ketchup, stone ground mustard, and hot sauce or a selection of your favorite condiments. We love easy Homemade Barbecue Sauce *(recipe page 64).*

Pint-Size

CHICKEN 'N' WAFFLES

makes 30

Who doesn't love chicken and waffles? We certainly do, especially when they're topped with rich, sweet homemade honey butter. Just make sure you're not too hungry when you make this classic soul food dish, or you may end up with a stomachache and nothing to feed your guests!

10 chicken tenders, each cut into 3 equal pieces
2 cups buttermilk
1/4 cup (1/2 stick) salted butter, softened
2 1/2 tablespoons honey, plus extra for drizzling
30 mini waffles, or 3 1/2 Belgian waffles, cut into 30 (1-inch) pieces
1 1/2 cups all-purpose flour
1 tablespoon garlic powder
2 teaspoons smoked paprika
1 teaspoon salt
1/2 teaspoon onion powder
1/2 teaspoon black pepper
2 cups vegetable oil

1. Place chicken in a bowl and cover with buttermilk. Stir gently, cover, and refrigerate. *{Tip: Soaking the chicken in the buttermilk several hours or overnight will help the breading adhere better when frying.}*
2. To prep the honey butter, whisk together butter and honey in a small bowl to combine.
3. Preheat oven to 375°F. Place waffles on a baking sheet and toast for 12 to 15 minutes.
4. In a small shallow dish stir together flour, garlic powder, paprika, salt, onion powder, and black pepper. Heat oil in a medium cast-iron skillet over medium-high heat. Remove chicken from buttermilk and dredge in flour mixture. Shake off excess and carefully drop breaded chicken into the hot oil. Fry for about 5 minutes on each side. Drain onto paper towels and season with salt.
5. Spread a teaspoon of honey butter onto each waffle and top with a piece of fried chicken. Finish with a drizzle of honey and serve warm.

A Little Menu

TINY FAIR FOOD PARTY

This fun menu combines two of our favorite things: mini food and fair food! Serve bite-size versions of these classic treats on sticks and party plates. They're perfect for birthday parties and outdoor get-togethers.

"Onion" Rings 25

Shallots thinly sliced, battered, fried, and served with Creamy Buttermilk Ranch Sauce

Bolinhos De Bacalhau 35

Shredded cod mixed with mashed potatoes and thyme, breaded and fried and served with zesty Lemon-Caper Dipping Sauce

Corn Dogs 69

Little smokeys, skewered onto toothpicks and dipped in corn dog batter with crumbled bacon and served with ketchup and yellow mustard

Chicken 'n' Waffles 70

Buttered mini waffles topped with small pieces of buttermilk-fried chicken tenders and a drizzle of sweet maple syrup

Mac 'n' Cheese Bites 85

Creamy mac 'n' cheese cut into small triangles, coated in panko bread crumbs, and deep-fried

Snickerdoodle Ice Cream Sandwiches 104

Small snickerdoodle cookies sandwiching vanilla ice cream and ground cinnamon, rolled in mini butterscotch chips

Funnel Cakes 120

Two-inch funnel cakes topped with whipped cream, chocolate sauce, and a cherry

A Little Menu

TINY BREAKFAST FOOD PARTY

Delicious for brunch or breakfast for dinner, these recipes are inspired by the most important meal of the day. Even the Cinnamon Spiced Cupcakes are sprinkled with candied bacon bits!

Savory Scones 13

Scones baked with crumbled feta, sun-dried tomatoes, and oregano

Chicken 'n' Waffles 70

Buttered mini waffles topped with small pieces of buttermilk-fried chicken tenders and a drizzle of sweet maple syrup

Stuffed French Toasts 75

Egg bread triangles filled with a mix of berry jam and mascarpone, soaked in a sweet cream-egg mixture, then rolled in crushed macadamia nuts and cornflakes, pan-fried, and served with a side of maple syrup

Country-Style Eggs Benedict 76

Bite-sized buttermilk biscuits, topped with breakfast sausage coins and fried quail eggs, finished with roasted garlic cheese sauce

Cinnamon Spiced Cupcakes 108

Spice cake baked in mini muffin tins, topped with peanut butter frosting and candied bacon bits

Homemade Pop Tarts 124

Pie dough cut into small rectangles and stuffed with a fruity strawberry-blueberry jam filling or delicious Nutella and marshmallow s'mores filling, baked, cooled, and covered in Royal Icing and sprinkles

Coffeecake Cocktails 146

Vanilla vodka, coffee liqueur, cream, and ground cinnamon, garnished with a crumbled coffeecake rim

Li'l STUFFED FRENCH TOASTS

makes 24

French toast is made even more irresistible thanks to a lovely blueberries-and-cream filling. The crumbly cornflake–macadamia nut coating adds a sweet flavor and light and crunchy texture to these tiny stuffed treats.

1. Place cheese, jam, and $^1/_2$ teaspoon of the cinnamon in a small bowl and stir to combine. Spread mixture over 3 of the bread slices and top with remaining slices. Cut each sandwich into 8 small triangles.
2. In a small shallow dish, whisk together eggs, milk, orange zest and juice, vanilla, and the remaining $^1/_2$ teaspoon cinnamon. Place cornflakes and macadamia nuts in the bowl of a food processor and process to a coarse meal; pour into another shallow dish. Dunk each bread triangle into egg mixture, let soak for 1 minute, flip, and let soak for an additional 30 seconds. Dredge triangles in cornflake mixture until fully coated.
3. Melt butter in a skillet over medium heat. Add half the triangles and let them brown and crisp, about 3 minutes. Flip and cook 3 minutes more. Remove from heat and cook the second batch. Serve warm with cocktail picks and maple syrup for dipping.

CREAMY BERRY FILLING

4 ounces mascarpone or cream cheese, softened
2 tablespoons blueberry jam
1 teaspoon cinnamon, divided

TOASTS

6 slices sourdough bread, crusts removed
3 eggs, lightly beaten
$^1/_4$ cup milk
Zest and juice of 1 orange
1 teaspoon vanilla extract
1 cup cornflakes
$^1/_2$ cup macadamia nuts
3 tablespoons butter

DIPPING SAUCE

1 cup pure maple syrup*

24 cocktail picks

** Pure maple syrup can be expensive. Pancake syrup is a tasty, affordable alternative.*

Itty-Bitty

COUNTRY-STYLE EGGS BENEDICT

makes 16

It's eggs Benedict like you've never seen. These fun bite-size breakfast treats are made with easy homemade Buttermilk Biscuits, breakfast sausage, teensy quail eggs, and creamy Roasted Garlic Cheese Sauce.

Biscuit dough, 1 (16-ounce) can store-bought or homemade (page 78)
$^{1}/_{2}$ pound breakfast sausage
3 tablespoons vegetable oil, divided
16 quail eggs, plus 1 or 2 chicken egg whites*

ROASTED GARLIC CHEESE SAUCE

2 teaspoons unsalted butter
1 head roasted garlic, mashed
2 teaspoons all-purpose flour
$^{3}/_{4}$ cup milk (whole or low fat)
2 ounces sharp white cheddar cheese, grated
Salt and pepper, to taste

** Quail eggs tend to have a high yolk-to-white ratio. Adding 1 or 2 chicken egg whites to the quail eggs and cooking them all together will ensure that you have enough whites between the yolks to form perfect sunny-side-up eggs.*

1. Preheat oven and bake biscuits according to package instructions (or as indicated on page 78). Cut sausage into 16 coins. Warm 1 tablespoon of the oil in a medium skillet over medium heat. Add sausages and cook for 4 to 5 minutes on each side; remove from heat.
2. Gently crack quail eggs into a small bowl and pour in chicken egg whites. Heat the remaining 2 tablespoons of oil in a large ovenproof skillet over medium heat. Carefully pour eggs into skillet and cook for 3 minutes. Reduce oven temperature to 350°F and place skillet in the oven. Bake for 3 to 5 minutes, or until whites have set. Gently transfer eggs in a single sheet from the skillet to a cutting board. Use a $1^{1}/_{2}$-inch circle cutter to cut eggs into 16 rounds, centering the cutter around a yolk so that each cut round looks like a little fried egg.
3. For the cheese sauce, melt butter in a small saucepan over medium heat. Add garlic and flour and whisk for 3 minutes. Add milk and whisk until no lumps remain and the mixture begins to thicken. Stir in cheese and season with salt and pepper. Simmer for 2 minutes more, or until sauce is smooth and creamy.
4. Slice each biscuit in half. Place a sausage coin over each biscuit half and top with a sunny-side-up quail egg and a drizzle of cheese sauce. Serve warm.

Breakfast sausage can be swapped for pieces of thick-cut bacon.

Homemade Goodness

→ PINT-SIZE BUTTERMILK BISCUITS ←

makes 8

These country-style buttermilk biscuits are quick and easy to make and are the perfect foundation for mini breakfast sandwiches and Country-Style Eggs Benedict (page 76). Of course, they're delicious simply slathered with jam or homemade Honey Butter (see step 2 on page 70) for a sweet treat.

1 cup all-purpose flour
1 teaspoon baking powder
$^1/_8$ teaspoon baking soda
$^1/_2$ teaspoon salt
$^1/_4$ teaspoon black pepper
$^1/_4$ cup ($^1/_2$ stick) cold unsalted butter, cubed
$^1/_3$ cup buttermilk
$^1/_4$ cup heavy cream, for brushing

1. Preheat oven to 425°F. Line a baking sheet with parchment paper.
2. Sift together flour, baking powder, baking soda, salt, and pepper in a mixing bowl. Using a pastry cutter, two knives, or your fingers, cut butter into flour mixture until it reaches a coarse, mealy texture. Add buttermilk and mix with your hands until dough just comes together.
3. Form dough into an 8- to 10-inch-wide disk about $^1/_4$ inch thick. Using a $1^1/_2$-inch circle cutter, cut out 8 biscuits and place on the prepared sheet. Brush tops of biscuits with cream and bake for 16 to 20 minutes, or until golden brown. Remove from oven and let cool slightly before serving.

A Tiny Party Trick

EASY MINI BAGUETTES

makes 24

Mini hamburger buns and slider rolls are widely available at grocery stores. But here's a fun trick for baking your own little baguettes for tiny sandwiches and subs.

All-purpose flour, for dusting
6 store-bought frozen rolls (such as Parker House), thawed

1. Preheat oven to 350°F. Line a baking sheet with parchment paper.
2. Dust a cutting board or other clean work surface with flour. Cut each roll into fourths. Using a rolling pin or your hands, roll each piece of dough into a 2-by-½-inch loaf and place on the prepared sheet. Bake for 12 to 15 minutes, or until golden brown and fluffy. Let cool. *{Tip: Rolls can be baked up to 3 days ahead and kept in an airtight container. Warm rolls in a 200°F oven for about 10 minutes before serving.}*

Shape frozen dough into rings and reduce the baking time by a few minutes to make your own mini bagels.

Mini BÁNH MÌ SANDWICHES

makes 24

Also known as a Vietnamese hoagie, *bánh mì* is a delicious Vietnamese street food that's quickly gaining popularity around the world. And it's easy to see why: these beef or pork sandwiches are topped with a sweet and tangy mix of condiments to please the palate. Either way, these itty-bitty edibles are sure to be a crowd pleaser.

MARINATED PORK BELLY

½ pound pork belly, thinly sliced
3 tablespoons soy sauce
2 tablespoons hoisin sauce
1 tablespoon rice wine vinegar
2 teaspoons sesame oil
1 teaspoon granulated sugar
1 tablespoon minced ginger
1 garlic clove, minced
1 green onion, thinly sliced
Black pepper, to taste

PICKLED CARROT-DAIKON SALAD

1 carrot, cut into matchsticks
½ cup daikon,* cut into matchsticks
1 cup rice wine vinegar
½ cup warm water
½ cup granulated sugar
1 teaspoon salt

FOR ASSEMBLING SANDWICHES

¼ cup mayonnaise
2 green onions, thinly sliced
2 ounces chicken liver or pork pâté
24 Easy Mini Baguettes (page 79), sliced lengthwise
1 small cucumber, thinly sliced
2 to 3 Serrano peppers, thinly sliced
½ bunch cilantro

** This large white radish is mild in flavor and packed with nutrients.*

1. Preheat oven to 350°F. Place pork belly in a medium mixing bowl. In a small bowl, whisk together all the marinade ingredients. Pour marinade over pork belly and stir to coat. Cover and refrigerate for 30 minutes.
2. In a small bowl, combine carrots and daikon. In another small bowl, stir together vinegar, warm water, sugar, and salt until ingredients are combined and sugar is dissolved. Pour mixture over vegetables and toss. Refrigerate for at least an hour, until vegetables have pickled. *{Tip: The pork belly and daikon-carrot mixture can be prepared until this point up to 2 days ahead.}* Grill over high heat for 1 to 2 minutes on each side.
3. Whisk together mayonnaise and green onions in a small bowl.
4. Spread a thin layer of pâté on the bottom half of each baguette and a layer of green-onion mayonnaise on the top half. Fill each roll with a little cucumber, pork belly, pickled carrot-daikon salad, peppers, and cilantro. Close sandwiches and serve.

For a veggie option, replace the pork belly with ½ pound cubed tofu and marinate as directed.

Tiny

FRIED TACOS

makes 24

These crunchy little tacos are easy to make and packed with flavor. Stuffed with a yummy shredded chicken filling or other favorites, they don't require silverware or a ton of napkins like regular-size tacos so often do. They're sure to be a hit at your next game-day get-together or poker night.

2 quarts vegetable oil, for frying
½ store-bought cooked rotisserie chicken
Juice of 1 lime
1 tablespoon ancho chili powder
2 teaspoons smoked paprika
1 teaspoon ground cumin
Salt and pepper, to taste
24 (3-inch) yellow corn tortillas*

TOPPINGS

¼ cup crema mexicana or sour cream
½ cup shredded iceberg lettuce
¼ cup crumbled cotija cheese,** or feta
Hot sauce, to taste

1. In a large pot, preheat oil to 375°F.
2. Remove skin and bones from the chicken and shred meat into a medium bowl. Add lime juice, chili powder, paprika, cumin, and salt and pepper and toss to combine. Place a big pinch of chicken mixture in the center of each tortilla.
3. Using tongs, gently fold each tortilla around filling and hold under the oil for a minute before releasing; let it fry for an additional 3 to 5 minutes, or until crisp and golden brown. Fry tacos a few at a time to avoid overcrowding. Drain on paper towels and season with salt to taste.
4. Gently hold each taco open and add toppings as desired.

For vegetarian tacos, stem and thinly slice 8 ounces (about 2 cups) cremini mushrooms; sauté until softened and then combine with remaining filling ingredients. For a dessert taco option, check out the Sweet Corn Ice Cream Tacos on page 129.

** If tiny tortillas are difficult to find, use a 3-inch circle cutter to cut mini tortillas out of larger ones.*

*** This firm, aged Mexican cheese can be grated or crumbled like Parmesan. It softens but doesn't melt when heated, making it an excellent garnish for tacos, beans, and chili.*

Snacky

MAC 'N' CHEESE BITES

makes 128

We love making mac 'n' cheese even more decadent by adding crumbled bacon to the mix and frying small portions into rich and creamy bites of goodness. Preparing the macaroni and cheese a day ahead allows the flavors to meld to perfection; chilling it ensures easy frying.

MACARONI AND CHEESE

1/2 pound small elbow macaroni
2 tablespoons unsalted butter
1 1/2 tablespoons all-purpose flour
1 cup buttermilk
1/2 cup grated Gruyère cheese
1/4 cup grated fontina cheese
2 teaspoons dry mustard
2/3 cup crumbled cooked bacon (from about 6 strips)
2 green onions, thinly sliced
Salt and pepper, to taste

FOR FRYING

1 quart vegetable oil
1 cup all-purpose flour
2 eggs, lightly beaten
1 1/2 cups panko bread crumbs*

** Panko bread crumbs are particularly airy, flaky, and wonderfully crunchy when fried. Originally from Japan, they are now widely available at most grocery stores.*

1. Fill a large pot with water and bring to a boil. Add macaroni, along with 3 1/2 tablespoons of salt, and stir. Boil pasta according to package instructions until al dente, stirring frequently. Drain and transfer to a large mixing bowl.
2. In a small saucepan over medium heat, melt butter. Whisk in flour and continue to whisk until mixture just begins to turn light golden brown, about 5 minutes. Whisk in buttermilk until no lumps remain and mixture thickens enough to coat the back of a spoon. Add cheeses and dry mustard and stir until fully incorporated and smooth. Pour cheese sauce over cooked macaroni and stir together. Fold in bacon and green onions until just combined. Season with salt and pepper. Pour into a greased 8-by-8-inch baking dish, cover with plastic wrap, and refrigerate overnight.
3. Preheat oil to 350°F. Cut chilled mac 'n' cheese into 1-inch squares; cut again on the diagonal into triangles. Place flour in a shallow dish, eggs in a second shallow dish, and panko in a third shallow dish. Lightly dredge mac 'n' cheese triangles in flour, shaking off excess. Dip floured triangles in eggs and then toss in panko until fully coated. Fry, in small batches, for 3 to 4 minutes, or until golden brown. Drain on paper towels, season with salt and pepper, and serve warm.

These versatile tidbits can be flavored with any mix-ins you like. Try 1/2 cup diced cooked ham instead of the bacon, along with 2 thinly sliced green onions and 1/2 cup diced roasted red bell peppers.

Teeny CHICKEN PARMESAN CROSTINI

makes 24

These bite-size antipasti are a playful take on the classic Italian American dinner. Accompanied by fresh Homemade Marinara (page 88), each bite explodes with flavor.

TOASTS

1 sourdough baguette, sliced into 24 (1/4-inch-thick) pieces
1/4 cup extra-virgin olive oil
Salt and pepper, to taste

CHICKEN PARMESAN

8 chicken tenders, each cut into 3 pieces
1 cup all-purpose flour
2 eggs, lightly beaten
1 cup Italian-style bread crumbs
1/4 cup extra-virgin olive oil
Salt and pepper, to taste
4 slices provolone cheese, each cut into 6 pieces

1 1/4 cups marinara, homemade (page 88) or store-bought

1. Preheat oven to 375°F. Brush baguette slices with oil and place on a nonstick sheet pan. Season with salt and pepper. *{Tip: You can make the toasts up to 3 days ahead to save time on the day of your get-together. After baking, store them in an airtight container.}*
2. Bake bread slices for 15 minutes, or until golden brown. Keep the oven on.
3. Place flour in a shallow dish, eggs in a second shallow dish, and bread crumbs in a third shallow dish. Dredge chicken in flour, then in eggs, and then in bread crumbs. Warm oil in a skillet over medium-high heat. Sauté chicken for 4 to 5 minutes on each side. Season with salt and pepper. Place chicken on a sheet pan and top each piece with a small slice of provolone. Bake for about 5 minutes, or until cheese melts. Spread about 1 tablespoon marinara on each toast and top with a piece of chicken. Top crostini with extra marinara and serve warm.

The Secret's in the Sauce

HOMEMADE MARINARA

makes 1¼ cups

This simple, all-purpose tomato sauce is delicious over pasta, meats, and seafood. Used as a dipping sauce or spread, it loads flavor onto sandwiches and appetizers, like the Teeny Chicken Parmesan Crostini on page 86.

1. Warm oil in a large pot over medium-high heat. Sauté onions, celery, and carrots for 4 to 6 minutes. Season with salt and pepper. Add basil, oregano, thyme, garlic, and bay leaf and sauté for another 2 minutes. Stir in tomato paste and lower heat to medium. Sauté for 5 minutes. Deglaze pan with wine and simmer for 2 minutes. *{Tip: Deglazing helps incorporate all the delicious brown bits on the bottom of the pan into the sauce. When you add the wine, use a wooden spoon to scrape up those little bits of flavor!}*
2. Add tomatoes and their juices and stir, gently crushing tomatoes with the back of a wooden spoon. Bring mixture to a boil and then lower heat and simmer, covered, for about 30 minutes. Transfer to a blender, discarding bay leaf, and puree until smooth. Return sauce to pot and simmer for 5 minutes more. *{Tip: Make the marinara up to 3 days ahead to save time on the day of your get-together.}*

3 tablespoons extra-virgin olive oil
¼ medium yellow onion, diced (about ½ cup)
½ celery stalk, diced
½ carrot, peeled and diced
Salt and pepper, to taste
¼ cup chopped fresh basil leaves
2 tablespoons chopped fresh oregano
1 tablespoon chopped fresh thyme
1 garlic clove, minced
1 bay leaf
½ tablespoon tomato paste
¼ cup red wine
14 ounces canned whole tomatoes, with liquid

HOMEMADE CHEESE SAUCE

makes about 1½ cups

A staple of French and Italian cuisine, this classic cheese sauce is basically just a fancy homemade Cheez Whiz! It's ideal for serving over nachos or fries and topping—or dunking—Mini Philly Cheesesteak Sandwiches (page 91).

1. Melt butter in a small saucepan over medium heat. Sprinkle in flour and whisk for about 2 minutes. Add milk and whisk until no lumps remain. Lightly season with salt and pepper. Once mixture thickens enough to coat a spoon, sprinkle in cheese, mustard, and cayenne pepper, stirring until melted and sauce is smooth.

2 tablespoons unsalted butter
2 tablespoons flour
1 cup milk (whole or low fat)
Salt and pepper, to taste
⅛ teaspoon dry mustard
Pinch cayenne pepper
⅔ cup grated sharp cheddar cheese

A Little Menu

TINY LUNCHBOX TREATS

Here's a collection of recipes that are particularly good either boxed up or wrapped up and tucked into lunch boxes, making for a special noontime treat.

Pajeon 29

Mini Korean-style seafood and vegetable pancakes served with Spicy Sesame Soy Sauce

Potato Samosas 32

Spiced potato and vegetable filling stuffed into pieces of dough and baked or fried and served with raita, a cucumber yogurt sauce

Beef Empanadas 42

Buttery pastries filled with seasoned ground beef, herbs, spices, and green olives

Deep-Dish Pizzas 60

Homemade pizza dough baked in mini tart shells and filled with Italian sausage and mozzarella, topped with tomato sauce and grated cheese

Philly Cheesesteak Sandwiches 91

Mini homemade baguettes stuffed with thinly sliced ribeye steak, caramelized bell peppers, and onions, complete with fancy homemade cheese sauce

Boston Cream Cakes 119

Layers of fluffy vanilla cake sandwich custard cream filling, topped with a decadent chocolate buttercream

Cinnamon-Sugar Palmiers 123

Homemade French puff pastry cookies filled with cinnamon-sugar, rolled, thinly sliced, baked, and then dipped in caramel sauce followed by melted chocolate and finished with a sprinkle of sea salt

Mini PHILLY CHEESESTEAK SANDWICHES

makes 24

Here's a fun take on the ever-popular Philadelphia classic, the enormous cheesesteak sandwich. Our recipe for tasty cheese sauce makes more than you'll need for topping the sandwiches—serve the extra on the side for dipping.

24 homemade Mini Baguettes (page 79) or mini rolls, halved
3½ tablespoons extra-virgin olive oil, divided
½ pound boneless rib-eye steak, thinly sliced
Salt and pepper, to taste
1 shallot, thinly sliced
½ green bell pepper, seeded and thinly sliced
1½ cups Homemade Cheese Sauce (page 88)*

* *If you prefer store-bought Cheez Whiz (as do most Philadelphians), go for it! Small slices of sharp provolone are another good alternative.*

1. Warm rolls in a 200°F oven for about 10 minutes.
2. Pour 1½ tablespoons of the oil into a medium heavy-bottom skillet over medium-high heat. Sear meat for about 2 minutes on each side; season with salt and pepper and transfer to a small bowl. Add the remaining 2 tablespoons oil into the same skillet and sauté shallots and peppers for about 5 minutes. Season with salt and pepper.
3. Layer a small amount of steak, peppers, and shallots on the bottom of each roll. Spread 1 teaspoon cheese sauce onto the top of each roll and gently press sandwiches closed. Serve the remaining cheese sauce on the side, for dipping the sandwiches.

Chapter 3

TINY DESSERT PARTY!

A Little Something Sweet

Little-Bitty
FUDGE PUPPIES

makes 24

Fudge puppies are a traditional fair food: toasty waffles dipped in chocolate and topped with whipped cream, crushed nuts, or other toppings. We've made them snack size and dipped them in crushed banana chips for added sweetness and crunch.

1½ cups sweet banana chips
1 cup dark or semisweet chocolate chips
24 mini waffles,* toasted
About 1 cup Sweet Whipped Cream (page 96) or store-bought whipped cream

**Mini waffles are available in the frozen-foods section of most supermarkets and grocery stores. They come in regular, whole wheat, cinnamon, and blueberry variations, to name a few. If you're a serious waffle lover, consider investing in a mini Belgian waffle maker.*

1. Place banana chips into the bowl of a food processor and pulse until coarsely ground. *{Tip: Alternatively, place chips in a plastic zip-top bag, seal it, and smash with a rolling pin.}* Pour crushed chips into a small shallow bowl.
2. Line a baking sheet with parchment paper. Melt chocolate chips in a double boiler over medium heat, stirring occasionally until smooth. *{Tip: Be careful not to let even a drop of water get into melting chocolate or it will seize up and become unusable}.* Partially dip each waffle into the melted chocolate, gently shaking off excess, and then dredge in the crushed banana chips until well coated. Place on the prepared sheet and let chocolate set for about 30 minutes. Serve fudge puppies with fresh Sweet Whipped Cream on top or on the side.

Once the chocolate has set, you can drop Mini Fudge Puppies into cellophane baggies for gifting or packing into lunchboxes. Just twist the bags closed and tie with a ribbon or baker's twine.

Homemade Toppings

SWEET WHIPPED CREAM

makes about 1 cup

What's dessert without a little freshly whipped cream?

1 cup heavy cream
2 tablespoons granulated sugar
1 teaspoon vanilla extract

1. Place all ingredients in a medium mixing bowl or the bowl of a stand mixer fitted with the whisk attachment and beat for 4 to 5 minutes, or until roughly doubled in volume and stiff peaks form. *{Tip: Check for stiff peaks by dipping a whisk or wooden spoon into the whipped cream and lifting it. Cream will stand up in stiff, slightly droopy peaks when whipped to perfection.}*

BLUEBERRY COMPOTE

makes about 3/4 cup

A compote is lovely mixture of fruit and sugar syrup, cooked down and served warm or cold. It makes a lovely topping for desserts like ice cream or the mini cheesecakes on page 99.

1 cup fresh or frozen blueberries
1/3 cup granulated sugar
2 tablespoons honey
1 tablespoon lemon juice
1/2 teaspoon cinnamon

1. Place all ingredients into a small saucepan and stir to combine.
2. Cook over medium-low heat and let simmer, stirring occasionally, for 15 minutes, or until blueberries have released juices and the mixture becomes a thick syrup. Let cool before serving.

You can swap strawberries, raspberries, or mixed fruit for the blueberries.

A Little Menu

TINY DESSERT PARTY

For special occasions or just for fun, make these bite-size desserts and invite friends over for a tasting party!

Fudge Puppies 94

Mini waffles dunked in melted chocolate and rolled in crushed banana chips

White Chocolate Cheesecakes 99

Baked in mini muffin tins and topped with Blueberry Compote

Mochi Ice Cream Balls 103

Yummy little Japanese confections filled with green tea ice cream

Homemade Hostess Cupcakes 107

Mini devil's food cupcakes filled with Marshmallow Fluff and dipped in a warm chocolate ganache, decorated with loops of icing

Candied Bacon Churros 113

Caramelized bacon mixed into churro batter, fried, and tossed in a light coating of cinnamon-sugar

Funnel Cakes 120

Two-inch funnel cakes topped with whipped cream, chocolate sauce, and a cherry

Fried Apple Pies 130

Three-inch fried pies stuffed with apple filling, fried hot, and served with a drizzle of Vanilla Icing

One-Bite

WHITE CHOCOLATE CHEESECAKES

makes 18

Easy to pick up and pop in your mouth, these pretty desserts are perfect for any party. We stir melted white chocolate into the creamy filling before scooping it into graham cracker crusts and topping it off with a drizzle of sweet and tangy blueberry compote.

CRUST

1½ cups graham cracker crumbs (from 6 whole sheets)
¼ cup granulated sugar
¼ cup (½ stick) unsalted butter, melted

CHEESECAKE FILLING

16 ounces cream cheese, softened
⅓ cup granulated sugar
2 eggs
1 egg yolk
1 tablespoon all-purpose flour
6 ounces white chocolate, melted
2 teaspoons vanilla extract
½ teaspoon salt

TOPPING

About ⅓ cup Blueberry Compote (page 96)

1. Preheat oven to 350°F. Combine crust ingredients in a mixing bowl. Press 1½ tablespoons of the mixture into each bottom of 18 mini cheesecake pans or mini muffin tins.
2. In a stand mixer fitted with the paddle attachment or using a hand mixer, beat cream cheese and sugar for 2 minutes until smooth and creamy. Scrape down the sides of the bowl. With the mixer running, add eggs and yolk, one at a time, scraping down the sides of the bowl after each addition. Stir in flour, white chocolate, vanilla, and salt until just combined and smooth. Pour filling into crusts and bake for 25 minutes, or until the centers have set.
3. Let cheesecakes cool completely before removing from pan. Top each cheesecake with 2 teaspoons of blueberry compote and serve. *{Tip: Both the cheesecakes and the compote can be made a few days ahead; assemble just before serving.}*

Blueberry Compote looks fancy but is quick and easy to make—see the how-to on page 96. For a quick alternative topping, sprinkle some mini chocolate chips (a.k.a. mini semisweet morsels); they're available next to regular chocolate chips in the baking aisle of most grocery stores.

Dainty

CHOCOLATE RASPBERRY TARTS

makes 24

Little buttery crusts hold a layer of raspberry jam topped with smooth chocolate ganache. Dust raspberries in edible glitter to add a fancy and fun touch to these sweet treats.

2 cups all-purpose flour
3 tablespoons granulated sugar
1/2 teaspoon salt
3/4 cup (1 1/2 sticks) cold unsalted butter, cut into small cubes
3 1/2 tablespoons cold water
1/4 cup seedless raspberry jam
1 cup semisweet chocolate chips
1 cup heavy whipping cream
24 fresh raspberries
2 tablespoons gold luster dust*

** This edible glitter can be bought at specialty cake- and craft-supply stores or online. You can achieve a similar sparkling effect by rolling the raspberries in lightly beaten egg whites and then in colored sanding sugar.*

1. Preheat oven to 350°F. Place flour, sugar, and salt into the bowl of a food processor and pulse three times to combine. Add butter and continue to pulse until a coarse meal forms. With the food processor running, add water and process until a dough forms. Transfer dough to a clean work surface and knead a few times until smooth.
2. Press 3 tablespoons of the dough into each of 24 1-inch square tart molds and prick the bottom and sides with a fork. *{Tip: Can't find square molds? Use a mini muffin tin.}* Freeze for 30 minutes, or until firm, to ensure the sides of the tart shells don't collapse while baking. Bake for 20 to 25 minutes, or until golden brown. Remove shells from molds to cool completely.
3. Brush a small amount of jam into the bottom of each tart shell. Place chocolate chips in a heatproof bowl. Bring cream to a simmer in a small saucepan and then pour over chocolate chips. Let sit for 2 minutes and then stir until chocolate is melted and smooth. Divide ganache evenly among tart shells and let set about 2 hours.
4. Place raspberries and luster dust in a mixing bowl. Gently toss until raspberries are fully coated. Once ganache has set, place a glittery raspberry atop each tart. *{Tip: Using tweezers is a great way to avoid fingerprints and smudges on the raspberries and tarts.}*

Pair these treats with Petite Raspberry Champagne Cocktails (page 139).

Mini
MOCHI ICE CREAM BALLS

makes 24

Mochi is a yummy Japanese confection made of soft, chewy, sweet rice-flour dough that is often filled with ice cream or fresh fruit. Commercial varieties are available at specialty grocery stores (try Trader Joe's and H Mart), but if you can find mochiko flour, it's easy to make this unusual dessert yourself.

- $1\frac{1}{2}$ cups green tea ice cream
- 1 cup granulated sugar
- 1 cup mochiko*
- 2 tablespoons green tea powder
- 1 cup cornstarch

** Mochiko is a Japanese sweet rice flour that can be found in Asian grocery stores and the specialty section of most supermarkets.*

1. Line a baking sheet with parchment paper. Form ice cream into 24 1-tablespoon balls, place 1 inch apart on prepared sheet, and freeze until firm, at least 1 hour.
2. In a medium saucepan, bring sugar and $\frac{1}{2}$ cup water to a boil, stirring occasionally. Add mochiko and continue to stir until a sticky dough forms. Reduce heat to medium-low and cook, stirring, for 8 to 10 minutes. Add green tea powder and stir to incorporate. Pour dough onto a clean surface generously dusted with cornstarch and spread dough with a wooden spoon. Top with a dusting of cornstarch and let it cool for 10 minutes.
3. Using a $2\frac{1}{2}$-inch circle cutter, cut out 24 mochi rounds. Dust off excess cornstarch. One at a time, place mochi in the palm of your hand and quickly wrap a prepared ice cream ball inside, pinching the dough to seal. *{Tip: Carefully seal each ball to ensure that no ice cream leaks through.}* Freeze for at least 1 hour before serving.

Green tea is a classic mochi ice cream flavor, but mango, strawberry, chocolate, or vanilla flavors are also delicious. Omit the green tea powder (if desired) and add food coloring to the mochi to match the color of your filling.

Tiny

SNICKERDOODLE ICE CREAM SANDWICHES

makes 24

Sweet little cinnamon-sugar-dusted snickerdoodle cookies are delicious. But they're even better sandwiched with vanilla ice cream studded with crunchy toffee bits.

SNICKERDOODLES

$2\frac{3}{4}$ cups all-purpose flour
$2\frac{1}{2}$ teaspoons cream of tartar
1 teaspoon baking soda
$\frac{1}{4}$ teaspoon salt
$\frac{3}{4}$ cup ($1\frac{1}{2}$ sticks) unsalted butter, softened
$\frac{1}{4}$ cup butter-flavored shortening*
$1\frac{3}{4}$ cups granulated sugar, divided
1 egg
2 egg whites
1 tablespoon ground cinnamon

FOR SANDWICHES

1 pint vanilla ice cream
2 cups toffee pieces

* *Butter-flavored shortening adds even more butter flavor to pastries. You can substitute regular vegetable shortening or even leaf lard.*

1. Preheat oven to 400°F. Sift together flour, cream of tartar, baking soda, and salt into a medium mixing bowl. Cream together butter, shortening, and $1\frac{1}{2}$ cups of the sugar with an electric hand mixer, about 3 minutes. Add egg and egg whites, one at a time, mixing and scraping down the sides of the bowl after each addition. Fold flour mixture into butter mixture until fully incorporated. Form dough into a disk, cover with plastic wrap, and refrigerate for 1 hour.

2. Line a baking sheet with parchment paper. In a small bowl, combine the remaining $\frac{1}{4}$ cup sugar and cinnamon. Form dough into 1-tablespoon balls and roll in cinnamon-sugar to coat. Place about 1 inch apart on the prepared sheet. Bake for 10 to 12 minutes, or until the edges just start to brown. Transfer cookies to a wire rack to cool completely.

3. Spread a spoonful of ice cream onto half the cookies and press the remaining cookies on top. Roll the sides of each sandwich in toffee pieces. Freeze sandwiches for at least 1 hour before serving. *{Tip: These will stay freshest if wrapped individually in plastic wrap and stored in an airtight container in the freezer.}*

It isn't hard to find volunteers for an ice-cream cookie sandwich assembly line.

Li'l

HOMEMADE HOSTESS CUPCAKES

makes 48

Here's a fun take on the iconic American dessert. These pint-size cupcakes are filled with Marshmallow Fluff instead of the traditional vanilla cream, adding a light, fluffy center to an already decadent dessert!

1. Preheat oven to 350°F. Place all the ingredients for the cupcake batter into a large mixing bowl and whisk together until fully combined. Line a mini cupcake tin with liners and fill each about two-thirds full.
2. Bake for 15 to 20 minutes, or until a toothpick inserted in the center of a cupcake comes out clean. Let cupcakes cool completely in the pan. Carefully remove cupcakes from liners and discard, if desired.
3. Scoop Marshmallow Fluff into a piping bag fitted with a small round tip. Pierce bottoms of cupcakes with the piping tip and fill each with about 1 teaspoon of Fluff.
4. To make the ganache, pour cream into a small saucepan and bring to a simmer over medium-low heat. Place chocolate chips in a medium heatproof bowl. Pour cream over top and let sit for 2 minutes. Gently stir melted chocolate and cream together with a wooden spoon until full incorporated. Let cool for 3 to 5 minutes. Dip tops of each cupcake in ganache, shaking off excess. Let the ganache set, about 30 minutes.
5. Load royal icing into a piping bag fitted with a small round tip (about 1 cm wide) and pipe a small row of loops across each cupcake. Let set 5 to 10 minutes before serving.

DEVIL'S FOOD CUPCAKES

1 cup all-purpose flour
2/3 cup cake flour
1 cup granulated sugar
1/2 cup unsweetened cocoa powder
1 teaspoon baking soda
3/4 teaspoon salt
1 1/4 cups buttermilk (regular or low fat)
1/2 cup vegetable oil
1/2 cup strong brewed coffee
2/3 cup semisweet chocolate, melted
1 1/2 teaspoons apple cider vinegar
1 teaspoon pure vanilla extract

FILLING

1 cup Marshmallow Fluff

CHOCOLATE GANACHE

1/2 cup heavy cream
1/2 cup semisweet chocolate chips

1/2 recipe Royal Icing, page 124*

** As you mix the icing, add up to an extra 1/2 cup of powdered sugar to stiffen it and make it easy to pipe in decorative loops.*

Two-Bite

CINNAMON SPICED CUPCAKES

makes 24

Peanut butter, cinnamon, and bacon. Believe it or not, these seemingly mismatched ingredients come together in perfect harmony—and are positively irresistible. (Bake these as regular-size cupcakes at your own risk.)

SPICE CAKE

2 cups cake flour
1 tablespoon cinnamon
2 teaspoons baking powder
½ teaspoon ground allspice
¼ teaspoon ground nutmeg
¼ teaspoon salt
¼ cup (½ stick) unsalted butter, softened
⅔ cup light brown sugar, packed
2 eggs
3 tablespoons molasses
¾ cup buttermilk

FROSTING

⅔ cup smooth peanut butter
8 ounces cream cheese, softened
¼ cup (½ stick) unsalted butter, softened
2½ cups sifted powdered sugar
1½ teaspoons vanilla extract

FOR TOPPING

½ cup Candied Bacon (page 110)*

** Optional, but highly recommended*

1. Preheat oven to 350°F. In a mixing bowl, sift together flour, cinnamon, baking powder, allspice, nutmeg, and salt.
2. With an electric mixer on medium speed, cream butter and brown sugar for 3 minutes, or until light and fluffy. Scrape down the sides of the bowl. With the mixer running, add eggs, one egg at a time, followed by molasses and buttermilk. Mix until just combined. Whisk dry mixture into wet mixture and stir until no lumps remain. Line mini muffin tins with mini cupcake liners and fill each two-thirds full. Bake for 20 to 25 minutes, or until a toothpick inserted in the center comes out clean. Let cool completely.
3. For the frosting, beat together peanut butter and cream cheese on medium speed for 3 minutes, or until smooth. Beat in butter. Add powdered sugar, ½ cup at a time, beating after each addition until fully incorporated. Scrape down the sides of the bowl and stir in vanilla. Scoop frosting into a piping bag fitted with a round tip. Pipe frosting onto each cupcake in a circle, beginning at the outside edge and working inward in a spiral, creating 2 to 3 layers. Top with a sprinkling of Candied Bacon.

The Ultimate Secret Weapon

CANDIED BACON

makes about 1/2 cup

Whether you're making deviled eggs, churros, cupcakes, or corn dogs (pages 14, 113, 108, and 69), candied bacon is a reliable way to turn any dish into a real crowd pleaser.

2 tablespoons vegetable oil
1/2 pound bacon, minced
1 1/2 tablespoons granulated sugar

1. Line a baking sheet with parchment paper.
2. Warm oil in a large skillet over medium-high heat. Add bacon and fry, stirring occasionally, for 6 to 8 minutes, or until crisp. Transfer to a paper towel and drain all but about 2 tablespoons of the bacon grease from the pan.
3. Return fried bacon bits to skillet and reduce heat to medium-low. Sprinkle sugar over top and stir. Continue stirring until sugar is melted and bacon is well coated, 3 to 5 minutes. Pour candied bacon onto the prepared sheet and spread in an even layer. Let cool and dry, about 30 minutes, before using. *{Tip: Candied bacon can be stored in an airtight container for up to 3 days. If it begins to get sticky, spread onto a nonstick skillet and dry out over medium-low heat, stirring occasionally.}*

Try swapping brown sugar for granulated sugar or mixing spices like cracked pepper or cayenne pepper with the sugar before adding to the skillet.

Homemade Toppings

DULCE DE LECHE

makes about 1 cup

Dulce de leche is a creamy, caramel-colored sauce that originated in Latin America. Pronounced *DOOL-say du LAY-chay*, this sweet treat is delicious poured over ice cream, spread between layers of cakes or cookies, or used for dipping and dunking. It can be bought premade, but all you need to make it yourself is a can of sweetened condensed milk.

1 (14 ounce) can sweetened condensed milk

1. Remove the label and wash the can. Using the prong on a can opener, poke 2 or 3 holes through the top of the can. The key is to break the seal so that pressure will have a release when the can is heated.
2. Place pierced can in a saucepan three-fourths full of water. Bring to a simmer over medium heat. Let it simmer for 2 to 2½ hours, being careful to add more water as needed to keep the saucepan three-fourths full. *{Tip: A few table-spoons of the sweetened condensed milk will escape into the simmering water as it cooks.}*
3. Remove can from saucepan and let it cool completely before opening. Pour into a small bowl and whisk until smooth. Use immediately or store refrigerated in an air-tight container.

For a thicker, darker dulce de leche, let it cook longer, 3 to 3½ hours.

Itty-Bitty
CANDIED BACON CHURROS

makes 24

Although it's untraditional, we like to make these mini Spanish doughnuts with salty-sweet candied bacon bits mixed into the batter before deep-frying them to perfection. A warm bowl of Nutella is our favorite dipping sauce, but you can pair your churros with caramel sauce, dulce de leche, sweet whipped cream—or all three.

1 quart vegetable oil, for frying

BATTER

2 tablespoons unsalted butter
½ tablespoon granulated sugar
¼ teaspoon salt
¾ cup all-purpose flour
2 eggs
½ cup Candied Bacon (page 110)*

FOR TOPPING AND DIPPING

½ cup granulated sugar
2 tablespoons ground cinnamon
⅔ cup dulce de leche (homemade, page 111, or store bought), warmed
⅔ cup Nutella, stirred
⅔ cup Sweet Whipped Cream (page 96) or store-bought whipped cream, if desired

* *Optional, but highly recommended*

1. In a large pot, preheat oil to 350°F. Place ½ cup water, butter, sugar, and salt in a medium saucepan and bring to a boil. With a wooden spoon, stir in flour until a dough forms, 3 to 5 minutes. Reduce heat to medium-low and cook for about 2 minutes, or until batter is thick and sticky. Remove from heat and beat in eggs, one at a time, until fully incorporated. Fold in candied bacon.
2. Scoop batter into a piping bag fitted with a small star tip. Pipe batter directly into the oil, cutting it into 2-inch segments with kitchen scissors to create short, skinny pieces. Fry in small batches for 2 to 3 minutes on each side, or until golden brown. Transfer to paper towels to drain.
3. In a big shallow bowl or baking dish, combine sugar and cinnamon. Toss hot churros in cinnamon-sugar and serve with warmed dulce de leche and Nutella for dipping. Top with whipped cream if desired.

Snack-Size ÉCLAIRS

makes 32

Éclairs are already dainty in their regular form, but when "petiter," these pastries are even sweeter. What's more, they're easier to make than you might think. Bake fluffy strips of dough, fill them with pastry cream, and dip them in melted chocolate for a magical dessert.

3 tablespoons unsalted butter
1 teaspoon salt
1 cup all-purpose flour
3 eggs
About $\frac{1}{2}$ cup Super-Fancy Pastry Cream (page 117)
$\frac{1}{2}$ cup semisweet chocolate, melted

1. Preheat oven to 400°F. Line two baking sheets with parchment paper; set aside.
2. Place 1 cup water, butter, and salt in a medium saucepan and bring to a boil. Add flour and stir with a wooden spoon for 3 minutes, or until a sticky dough forms. Transfer dough to the bowl a stand mixer fitted with a paddle attachment and beat for 2 minutes to release some of the steam in the dough. Add eggs, one at a time, mixing and scraping down the sides of the bowl after each addition. Scoop dough into a piping bag fitted with a small round tip (about $\frac{1}{4}$ inch wide) and pipe $1\frac{1}{2}$-inch strips of dough onto one of the prepared sheets, leaving about 1 inch between them. Bake for 15 to 20 minutes, or until éclairs have puffed and turned golden brown. Let cool.
3. Scoop pastry cream into a clean piping bag fitted with a tiny round tip. Insert tip into the bottom or side of each éclair and squeeze in pastry cream to fill.
4. Dip tops of éclairs in melted chocolate, shaking off excess, and place onto the second prepared sheet to let chocolate set, about 1 hour.

For piping tips and tricks, see page 55.

A Little Menu

TINY FOOD PARTY FOR KIDS

Miniature foods are fun to make with (and for) little ones. Here's a selection of irresistible recipes that are a real treat for children or anyone who's young at heart.

Deep-Dish Pizzas 60

Homemade pizza dough baked in mini tart shells, filled with Italian sausage and mozzarella, and topped with tomato sauce and grated cheese

Corn Dogs 69

Little smokeys, skewered onto toothpicks and dipped in corn dog batter with crumbled bacon and served with ketchup and yellow mustard for dipping

Mac 'n' Cheese Bites 85

Creamy mac 'n' cheese cut into small triangles, coated in panko bread crumbs, and deep-fried

Snickerdoodle Ice Cream Sandwiches 104

Small snickerdoodle cookies sandwiching vanilla ice cream and ground cinnamon, rolled in mini butterscotch chips

Homemade Pop Tarts 124

Pie dough cut into small rectangles and stuffed with a fruity strawberry-blueberry jam filling or delicious Nutella and marshmallow s'mores filling, baked, cooled, and covered in Royal Icing and sprinkles

Coconut Cakes 133

Light and fluffy coconut cakes coated with a simple vanilla frosting and finished with lightly toasted shredded coconut

Ginger-Mint Lemonades 149

A kid-friendly version of the refreshing adult cocktail, with freshly squeezed lemonade and ginger simple syrup, stirred together with freshly muddled mint and ice

A Tiny Food Party Trick

⟼ SUPER-FANCY PASTRY CREAM ⟻

makes 2 cups

Homemade pastry cream is a dessert-party staple. Light yet rich, it is one of the best fillings for tarts, layer cakes, éclairs, cannolis, and other treats.

- 1 cup milk
- ½ cup granulated sugar
- ¼ teaspoon salt
- 2 tablespoons cornstarch
- 3 egg yolks
- 1½ tablespoons vanilla extract
- 1 cup Sweet Whipped Cream (page 96) or store-bought whipped cream

1. In a saucepan, whisk together all ingredients except whipped cream. Bring to a simmer over medium heat, stirring frequently. Simmer for 5 minutes, or until mixture thickens enough to coat the back of a spoon.
2. Strain mixture through a fine sieve into a medium mixing bowl and nest bowl in an ice bath to cool completely, stirring occasionally. Gently fold whipped cream into mixture until fully incorporated. *{Tip: Folding rather stirring will keep the pastry cream light and fluffy. Using a rubber spatula, lift the mixture at the bottom of the bowl up to the top with a gentle circular motion.}*
3. If the pastry cream is still lumpy, pass it through a fine sieve again and stir in 2 tablespoons of melted butter. This will remove the cooked yolk bits as well as give the pastry cream a smoother, glossier texture.

For a quick fix, use the super-fast Custard Cream recipe on page 119.

Baby

BOSTON CREAM CAKES

makes 16

Made with layers of fluffy vanilla cake, custard cream filling, and decadent chocolate buttercream, Boston cream pie is an irresistible dessert with a misleading name—it's really a cake! Or, in the case of this recipe, it's a bunch of adorable cakelets.

VANILLA CAKE

2 cups all-purpose flour
$2\frac{1}{2}$ teaspoons baking powder
$\frac{1}{4}$ teaspoon salt
1 cup (2 sticks) unsalted butter,* softened
$1\frac{3}{4}$ cups plus 1 tablespoon granulated sugar
4 eggs, at room temperature
$1\frac{1}{2}$ cups buttermilk
$1\frac{1}{2}$ tablespoons vanilla extract

CHOCOLATE BUTTERCREAM

$\frac{1}{2}$ cup (1 stick) unsalted butter, softened
$3\frac{1}{2}$ cups powdered sugar, sifted
4 ounces semisweet chocolate, melted
3 tablespoons milk

CUSTARD CREAM

$\frac{1}{2}$ cup Sweet Whipped Cream (page 96), or store-bought whipped cream
1 cup prepared vanilla pudding

** Use a fresh, good-quality butter (such as Kerrygold or Plugrá), because the higher fat content makes for a richer cake. Fresh butter should feel firm and smell lightly sweet.*

1. Preheat oven to 350°F. Grease two 9-inch cake pans and line pans with parchment paper.
2. Sift together flour, baking powder, and salt. With a mixer, cream together butter and sugar for about 3 minutes. With the mixer running, add eggs, one at a time, scraping down the sides of the bowl after each addition. Beat half the dry mixture into the butter mixture, then add the buttermilk and, lastly, the remaining dry mixture. Stir in vanilla. Divide the batter evenly between the prepared pans. Bake for 25 minutes, or until cakes are golden brown and a toothpick inserted in the center comes out clean. Let cool completely, about 45 minutes. Remove cakes from pans and refrigerate for 1 hour. *{Tip: Chilled cakes are easy to frost because the crumbs stay in place.}* Slice each cake in half lengthwise. Using a $1\frac{1}{2}$- to 2-inch circle cutter, cut out 48 cake rounds.
3. For the buttercream, whip butter in the bowl of a stand mixer fitted with the paddle attachment until light and fluffy. With the mixer running, add powdered sugar, $\frac{1}{2}$ cup at a time, beating after each addition. Add chocolate, then milk, and beat until smooth.
4. For the custard cream, fold whipped cream into pudding and transfer mixture to a piping bag fitted with a $\frac{1}{2}$-inch round tip. Squeeze a small amount onto 16 cake rounds and top each with another cake round, followed by another dollop of pastry cream. Spread a layer of buttercream onto the remaining cake rounds and place them, frosted side up, on top of the cakes.

Teensy

FUNNEL CAKES

makes 16

Golden brown and dusted with powdered sugar, giant plate-size funnel cakes can be found at carnivals, fairs, and sporting events. Treat your friends to a daintier version of this popular snack, served with a spread of your favorite toppings.

1. In a large heavy-bottom pot over medium-high heat, warm oil to 350°F. In a medium bowl, sift together flour, granulated sugar, cinnamon, baking powder, and salt. Whisk in milk and egg until no lumps remain and a thick batter has formed. *{Tip: The thicker the batter, the easier it will be to handle while frying. If your batter seems a bit runny, stir in flour, a tablespoon at a time, until it has a frosting-like consistency.}*
2. Carefully pour batter into a piping bag fitted with a small, round tip (or a resealable plastic bag with one corner snipped off). Pipe batter into oil with a small circular motion to create 3-inch cakes. Fry cakes for 2 to 3 minutes, gently flip them, and fry for an1 additional minute. Transfer to paper towels to drain.
3. Dust the cakes with powdered sugar and finish with toppings of your choice. Serve immediately.

1 quart oil, for frying
1 cup all-purpose flour
$1\frac{1}{2}$ tablespoons granulated sugar
$1\frac{1}{2}$ teaspoons ground cinnamon
$\frac{1}{2}$ teaspoon baking powder
$\frac{1}{2}$ teaspoon salt
$\frac{1}{2}$ cup milk (whole or low fat)
1 egg
$\frac{1}{2}$ cup powdered sugar, sifted

SUGGESTED TOPPINGS

Sliced strawberries
Blueberries
Chocolate sauce
Caramel sauce
Chopped peanuts
Mini chocolate chips
Whipped cream (see page 96 for homemade)
Nutella, stirred until smooth
Cherries, fresh or maraschino

Petite

CINNAMON-SUGAR PALMIERS

makes 24

These classic French pastries are traditionally jumbo-size treats and, aptly, often sold in American bakeries as "elephant ears." We dip our tiny version in gooey caramel and salted semisweet chocolate.

PALMIERS

1/2 cup granulated sugar

2 tablespoons ground cinnamon

1 sheet store-bought frozen puff pastry, thawed and cut in half

1/4 cup (1/2 stick) unsalted butter, melted

CARAMEL SAUCE

1/2 cup granulated sugar

1/4 cup light brown sugar

2 tablespoons light corn syrup

1/4 cup (1/2 stick) unsalted butter, cut into small cubes

1/3 cup heavy cream

SALTED CHOCOLATE

1 cup semisweet chocolate chips

2 tablespoons sea salt flakes

1. Preheat oven to 400°F. Line two baking sheets with parchment paper.
2. In a small bowl, toss sugar and cinnamon to combine. Brush both pieces of puff pastry with melted butter and coat evenly with cinnamon-sugar. Roll both long sides of each pastry toward the center of the sheet, creating two coils. Cut into 1/4-inch-thick slices and place 2 inches apart on one of the prepared sheets. Bake for 15 to 20 minutes, or until puffed and golden brown.
3. For the caramel sauce, combine sugars and corn syrup in a small pot over medium heat. When the temperature reaches 240°F, begin whisking in the butter, a few cubes at a time. Carefully whisk in cream. *{Tip: Watch out when whisking in the cream; the mixture will bubble up quickly at first.}* Remove from heat. Dip each palmier in caramel to coat about two-thirds of the pastry. Place on the second prepared sheet to set.
4. Melt chocolate chips in a double boiler over medium heat. Dip palmiers in melted chocolate to coat the caramel and place them back on sheet. Sprinkle sea salt flakes over palmiers. Let chocolate set completely before serving, about 1 hour.

Serve these delicate, lightly salty-sweet snacks at brunch or a cocktail party.

Mini

HOMEMADE POP TARTS

makes 24 (12 of each flavor)

These freshly baked bite-size treats are fun for kids and adults alike. We like to make two flavors: strawberry-blueberry and s'mores. Feel free to substitute your favorite fruit flavors.

1 recipe homemade pie dough (page 126) or store bought, chilled

FRUIT FILLING

1 cup hulled and chopped strawberries

½ cup blueberries

½ cup granulated sugar

2 tablespoons honey

S'MORES FILLING

¾ cup Nutella

¾ cup marshmallow crème

EGG WASH

1 egg, lightly beaten

¼ cup heavy cream, plus more for brushing pastries

ROYAL ICING

1 egg white

1¼ cups powdered sugar, sifted

1 teaspoon vanilla extract

Sprinkles, for decorating

1. Preheat oven to 375°F. Line two baking sheets with parchment paper.
2. Combine fruit filling ingredients and 3 tablespoons water in a medium pot over medium heat; stir. Gently mash berries with the back of a wooden spoon and simmer, stirring frequently, for 30 to 40 minutes, or until filling has thickened. Let cool.
3. Cut chilled dough into 4 equal pieces. Roll 2 pieces into equal rectangles about 3 by 8 inches. Fill a piping bag with Nutella and a second piping bag with marshmallow crème. Onto one of the rectangles, pipe rows of Nutella ½ inch apart. Pipe rows of marshmallow crème on top.
4. To make the egg wash, whisk together egg and heavy cream. Using a pastry brush, carefully brush egg wash onto dough between the rows of filling. Gently lay the second dough rectangle over top and press around each mound of filling. *{Tip: This is the same method used for homemade ravioli.}* Cut 1-by-1½-inch rectangles with a pizza cutter (you should have 12 tarts) and press the back of a fork along the edges to seal. Place tarts on one of the prepared sheets and brush lightly with cream. Cut 3 tiny slits in the top of each tart. Bake for 12 to 15 minutes, or until golden brown. Place on wire racks to cool completely. Repeat the process with the remaining two slabs of dough and the cooled fruit filling to make 12 fruit-filled tarts.
5. For the icing, in a medium mixing bowl or the bowl of a stand mixer, beat egg white on medium-high speed for 2 minutes, or until light and frothy. Add powdered sugar, ¼ cup at a time, until mixture is thick and smooth. Add vanilla and beat for 1 minute more. Spread icing onto pastries with an offset spatula or your fingers. Top with sprinkles.

A Tiny Food Party Trick

EASY-AS-PIE DOUGH

makes 12 to 16 ounces

Use this simple pie dough to make treats like Homemade Pop Tarts (page 124) and Fried Apple Pies (page 130). Cream cheese is the secret ingredient that increases the dough's elasticity, so that it's smooth and easy to handle, and also makes it extra flaky and delicious when baked.

2 cups all-purpose flour
1/4 teaspoon baking powder
1/4 teaspoon salt
3/4 cup cold unsalted butter, cut into cubes
1/4 cup cold cream cheese, cut into cubes
2 tablespoons ice water

1. In a medium mixing bowl, sift together flour, baking powder, and salt. Add butter and cream cheese and cut into dry ingredients with a pastry knife or your fingers until fine crumbles are formed.
2. Add ice water and, using your hands, gently work mixture until dough just comes together. Form dough into a disk, wrap with plastic wrap, and refrigerate until ready to use.

Try adding a teaspoon of apple cider vinegar to your pie dough in step 2, along with the ice water. It helps prevent the formation of gluten, resulting in a tender, flaky crust.

A Sweet and Savory Treat

HOMEMADE CANDIED CORN

makes about ½ cup

No, this recipe isn't for the addictively sweet Halloween candy. It's for something even better! Candied corn-off-the-cob is a tasty snack all on its own and also makes a lovely, lightly sweet topping for salads and savory dishes as well as desserts like ice cream.

½ cup sugar
Kernels from 1 ear of corn

1. Preheat oven to 300°F. Line a baking sheet with parchment paper. Place sugar and ½ cup water in a skillet over medium heat. Stir until sugar is dissolved. Stir in corn and simmer for 30 minutes.
2. Drain liquid and transfer corn to the prepared sheet. Bake for 5 minutes, just to dry kernels slightly. Remove from oven and let cool.

Teeny

→ SWEET CORN ICE CREAM TACOS ←

makes 12

Here's a fun, chocolate-less version of the Choco-Taco. Made with homemade Sweet Corn Ice Cream and topped with real Candied Corn, this sweet and salty snack will get your taste buds going.

TACO SHELLS

1 quart vegetable oil for frying

12 3-inch corn tortillas or larger corn tortillas cut to size

Salt, to taste

SWEET CORN ICE CREAM

2 ears sweet corn, kernels cut from cobs

1¼ cups heavy cream

¾ cup whole milk

⅔ cup sugar

4 egg yolks

¼ teaspoon salt

1 batch Candied Corn (page 127)

1. In a large pot over high heat, preheat oil to 375°F. Using a 2½- to 3-inch circle cutter, cut rounds from the tortillas. Fold each in half, pinch closed with tongs, and fry for 3 minutes before releasing tongs and letting fry for an additional 3 to 4 minutes. Drain on paper towels, season with salt, and repeat until all tortilla rounds have been fried.
2. For the ice cream, place kernels in a medium heavy-bottom saucepan. Add cream, milk, and half the sugar. Stirring occasionally, bring the mixture to a simmer for about 30 minutes. Pour it into a blender and puree until almost smooth. Strain mixture through a fine sieve, discarding any solids. Return mixture to the saucepan and bring it back up to a simmer. In a medium bowl, whisk together the egg yolks, salt, and remaining sugar. Whisk about ½ cup of the cream mixture into the yolk mixture, then pour tempered yolk mixture into the remaining cream mixture, whisking to avoid scrambling. Let mixture thicken (enough to coat the back of a spoon) and then strain through a fine sieve into a medium mixing bowl. Cover and place in the refrigerator until chilled, about 2 hours. Pour base into an ice cream maker and freeze. Scoop ice cream into an airtight container and place in freezer until ready to use.
3. Scoop a spoonful of ice cream into each prepared shell. Top each taco with a sprinkle of candied corn. Serve immediately.

Tiny

FRIED APPLE PIES

makes 18

Because their delicious apple filling is all sealed up—wrapped in dough like hand pies or campfire pies, but bite-size—these sweet little pies are perfect finger food. They transport easily, so you can take them to parties or potlucks. Or pack a few into your lunch for a sweet snack.

PIE FILLING

2 granny smith apples, peeled, cored, and diced
3 tablespoons granulated sugar
2 tablespoons fresh lemon juice
½ tablespoon minute tapioca
½ teaspoon cinnamon
½ teaspoon nutmeg
⅛ teaspoon allspice
⅛ teaspoon salt

Pie dough (store bought or homemade, page 126), chilled
1 quart vegetable oil, for frying

EGG WASH

1 egg, lightly beaten
¼ cup heavy cream

ICING

1 cup powdered sugar, sifted
2 tablespoons buttermilk
1 teaspoon vanilla extract

1. Place filling ingredients in a large bowl and toss until well combined. Cut chilled dough into 2 equal pieces. Roll into equal rectangles about ¼ inch thick. Onto one of the rectangles, place spoonfuls of filling (about 2 tablespoons each) in rows ½ inch apart. Place pies in the refrigerator and chill for 30 minutes.
2. To make the egg wash, whisk together egg and heavy cream. Using a pastry brush, carefully brush egg wash onto dough between the rows of filling. Gently lay the second dough rectangle over top and press around each mound of filling. Cut 3-by-1-inch rectangles with a pizza cutter and press the back of a fork along the edges to seal.
3. Preheat oil to 375°F. Carefully begin frying pies, a few at a time, for 7 to 8 minutes or until golden brown. Drain pies on paper towels and allow to cool.
4. Stir together the icing ingredients in a small bowl until smooth. Drizzle icing over pies and serve.

Cute Li'l

COCONUT CAKES

makes 12

These mini cakes are light, fluffy, and bursting with a sweet coconut flavor. How awesome would it be to serve these little guys at a birthday party? That way everyone gets his or her own little cake!

COCONUT CAKE
- 3 cups cake flour
- 1 teaspoon baking powder
- 1/2 teaspoon baking soda
- 1/4 teaspoon salt
- 1 cup (2 sticks) unsalted butter, softened
- 1 3/4 cups granulated sugar
- 4 eggs
- 1 cup coconut milk
- 1 teaspoon coconut extract*

VANILLA BUTTERCREAM FROSTING
- 1 cup (2 sticks) unsalted butter, softened
- 7 cups powdered sugar, sifted
- 1/3 cup plus 1 tablespoon milk
- 1 1/2 teaspoons vanilla extract

TOPPING
- 2 cups (sweetened) shredded coconut, lightly toasted**

** Coconut extract is available in the baking aisle of most grocery stores. You can substitute pure vanilla extract.*

*** Spread coconut on a baking sheet in a single layer. Bake at 350°F for 6 to 8 minutes, stirring every 2 or 3 minutes, until golden. Let cool.*

1. Preheat oven to 350°F. For the cake, sift flour, baking powder, baking soda, and salt into a medium mixing bowl.
2. Using a hand mixer or stand mixer, cream butter until light and fluffy, about 2 minutes. Scrape down sides of bowl and, with motor running, add sugar 1/2 cup at a time until fully incorporated and mixture is light and fluffy. Beat in eggs, one at a time, until well combined. Add flour mixture and coconut milk in three alternating additions, mixing until just combined. Stir in coconut extract and pour batter into two baking sheets lined with parchment paper and lightly greased. Bake for 25 to 30 minutes, or until a toothpick inserted into the center of the cake comes out clean. Let cakes cool completely.
3. For the frosting, use a hand mixer or stand mixer to cream butter, about 2 minutes. Add half the sugar (3 1/2 cups), 1/2 cup at a time, beating after each addition. Beat milk into frosting mixture before adding remaining sugar 1/2 cup at a time. Scrape down sides of the bowl, add vanilla, and beat 1 minute more, or until light and fluffy.
4. Using a 2- or 2 1/2-inch circle cutter, cut 24 cake rounds from each sheet pan. Spread an even layer of frosting over a cake round and top with another cake round to make a thick two-layer cake. Repeat for remaining cake rounds. Add a thin coating of frosting around sides and tops of each cake and set onto a sheet pan lined with parchment. *{Tip: Called a crumb coat, this thin coating of frosting chilled on cakes makes it easy to add a second layer of frosting because it keeps the crumbs in place.}* Place cakes in fridge to chill, about 2 hours. Spread another even layer of frosting around each cake and coat sides with toasted coconut before serving.

Chapter 4

TINY COCKTAIL PARTY!

Darling Drinks

Itty-Bitty BLOODY MARYS

makes 12

Our version of this classic American favorite uses *soju* (Korean rice wine) instead of vodka for a smoother, milder flavor. Garnish bacon-rimmed cocktail glasses with pickled green beans and cute little crispy fried quail eggs to turn this cocktail into a great happy hour drink and anytime snack.

2½ cups soju
2½ cups tomato juice
¼ cup Worcestershire sauce
3 tablespoons Sriracha hot sauce
2 limes, zested and juiced
2½ teaspoons black pepper

GARNISHES

¼ cup honey
½ cup crumbled bacon
24 pickled green beans
12 hard-boiled, breaded, and fried quail eggs (see page 16)
12 toothpicks

1. Place first 6 ingredients into a large pitcher over ice. Stir until well mixed. Set aside to chill.
2. Pour honey onto a small, shallow plate and spread it around. Rim each glass with a thin layer of honey followed by the crumbled bacon. Place 2 green beans into each glass and pour in chilled liquid. Skewer quail eggs onto toothpicks and place over each cocktail. Serve.

For a truly awesome savory-sweet garnish, rim cocktail glasses first in honey and then in crumbled bacon!

Petite

RASPBERRY CHAMPAGNE COCKTAILS

makes 12

A honey-sweetened raspberry-vodka puree is the secret that adds a lovely rosy blush to these elegant little sparkling cocktails.

1½ cups fresh raspberries
3 tablespoons granulated sugar
1 tablespoon honey
1½ cups vodka, divided
1 (750 ml) bottle Champagne or sparkling wine, chilled
1 cup Chambord, divided

GARNISH
12 fresh raspberries

1. Place raspberries, sugar, honey, and ½ cup of the vodka into a blender. Puree until smooth. Pour mixture through a fine sieve into a small pitcher. Pour remaining vodka into the raspberry mixture and stir.
2. Divide puree mixture among 12 small glasses. Pour the Champagne over each glass and top off with a small amount of Chambord.
3. Drop a fresh raspberry into each glass and serve.

Dainty

PINEAPPLE UPSIDE-DOWN CAKES

makes 12

Serve shooters of this lovely cake-inspired cocktail topped with a swirl of whipped cream. It's a fun way to drink your dessert!

1 cup sweet bourbon, such as Maker's Mark
$1\frac{1}{2}$ cups pineapple juice
$\frac{1}{4}$ cup triple sec
2 teaspoons vanilla extract

GARNISH

Sweetened Whipped Cream (store-bought or homemade, page 96)

1. Fill a large shaker with ice. Add bourbon, pineapple juice, triple sec, and vanilla. *{Tip: You may need to do this in several batches if you have a smaller shaker.}* Shake until cocktail is completely mixed and frosty cold.
2. Divide among 12 small glasses or shooters. Place whipped cream into a piping bag fitted with a star tip and top off each drink with a dollop of whipped cream.

For piping tips and tricks, see page 55.

Mini ORANGE CREAMSICLES

makes 12

Another dessert-turned-awesome-cocktail is our version of the popular frozen treat, the orange creamsicle. It's always fun drinking your way through dessert!

- $1\frac{1}{4}$ cups vanilla vodka
- $\frac{1}{4}$ cup triple sec
- $1\frac{1}{2}$ cups orange soda
- $\frac{1}{2}$ cup vanilla ice cream

GARNISH

- $\frac{1}{4}$ cup honey
- $\frac{1}{2}$ cup granulated sugar
- Zest of 2 oranges

1. Place vodka, triple sec, soda, and ice cream into a large bowl and stir until ice cream just melts.
2. Pour honey onto a small shallow plate and spread it around. Rim 12 small glasses with a thin layer of honey. In another small shallow dish, stir to combine sugar and zest. Dip each honey-rimmed glass into the sugar-zest mixture.
3. Ladle ice-cream mixture into the prepared glasses and serve.

Lighten up this drink by using sugar-free soda and fat-free ice cream and rimming the glasses with nothing but fresh orange zest.

A Little Menu

TINY COCKTAIL PARTY

Here's a collection of some of our favorite classic cocktail party foods made miniature. They're fun, flavorful, and easy to eat sans silverware. Pair these recipes with lovely Lemon-Lime Fizzes or your cocktail of choice.

Caprese Skewers 10

Small mozzarella balls sliced and sandwiched between sliced cherry tomatoes and fresh basil leaves, served with Sweet Balsamic Glaze

Kimchi Deviled Eggs 14

Kimchi pureed with egg yolks and a touch of mayonnaise, piped into quail eggs and topped with candied bacon bits

Seafood Cocktail Cups 26

Seafood salad with shrimp, bay scallops, sweet corn, red onion, cilantro lime juice, chipotle cocktail sauce, tossed, scooped into small cucumber cups, and topped with crumbled queso fresco

Coxinha 41

Shredded chicken, cream cheese, sweet corn, and green onions wrapped in dough and fried crispy hot

Chicken Parmesan Crostini 86

Bite-size pieces of chicken breasts breaded and pan-fried, topped with provolone, and marinara, and baked—then served on garlic crostini

Cinnamon Spiced Cupcakes 108

Spice cake baked in mini muffin tins, topped with peanut butter frosting and candied bacon bits

Lemon-Lime Fizzes 150

Light beer, citrus vodka, lemonade concentrate, lemon-lime soda, and fresh lemon and lime wheels, with a lime zest-and-sugar rim garnish

A Little Menu

TINY ASIAN FOOD PARTY

Serve these bite-size snacks for a sampling of Asian flavors. They're irresistible when accompanied by our fun recipe for delicious Korean-style Bloody Marys.

Kimchi Deviled Eggs 14

Kimchi pureed with egg yolks and a touch of mayonnaise, piped into quail eggs and topped with candied bacon bits

Pajeon 29

Savory Korean-style shrimp and green onion pancakes served with Spicy Sesame Soy Sauce

Bánh Mì Sandwiches 41

Marinated and grilled pork belly, homemade pickled carrots and daikon matchsticks, cilantro, sliced Serrano peppers, sliced snacking cucumbers, and pâté, all stuffed into mini baguettes

Mochi Ice Cream Balls 103

Yummy little Japanese confections filled with green tea ice cream

Bloody Marys 136

Spice cake baked in mini muffin tins, topped with peanut butter frosting and candied bacon bits

Little

COFFEECAKE COCKTAILS

makes 12

We love sipping on these rich, flavorful cocktails while munching Cinnamon-Sugar Palmiers and Candied Bacon Churros (pages 123 and 113).

1 cup coffee liqueur, such as Baileys
1/2 cup vanilla vodka
1 cup cream, light or heavy
1 teaspoon coffee extract*
1/2 teaspoon cinnamon

GARNISH
1/4 cup honey
1/2 cup finely crumbled coffeecake

**Coffee extract packs a strong punch. Because it's concentrated, it's great to use when you want the flavor of coffee without the additional liquid.*

1. Fill a large shaker with ice. Add coffee liqueur, vanilla vodka, cream, coffee extract, and cinnamon. *{Tip: You may need to do this in two batches if you have a smaller shaker.}* Shake until fully combined and chilled.
2. Pour honey onto a small shallow plate and spread around. Rim each glass with a thin layer of honey, followed by the crumbled coffeecake.
3. Divide coffee liqueur mixture among the honey-rimmed glasses and serve.

Bitty

GINGER-MINT LEMONADES

makes 12

Share this refreshing cocktail with friends at a tiny food party picnic on a hot summer day!

1 cup granulated sugar
1 cup water
1-inch piece of ginger, peeled and lightly smashed
$1\frac{1}{2}$ cups sweet bourbon, such as Maker's Mark
2 cups freshly squeezed lemon juice

GARNISH
1 bunch mint leaves

1. Place sugar, water, and ginger in a small saucepan over medium heat and simmer until sugar dissolves, stirring occasionally, 7 to 10 minutes. Set mixture aside and allow to cool completely.
2. Place a few mint leaves in each glass and fill with ice. Pour ginger-infused simple syrup, bourbon, and lemon juice into a large shaker filled with ice and shake until completely mixed. Divide among glasses and serve.

Substitute seltzer for the bourbon to make a round of fun fizzy drinks for the younger set.

Mini

LEMON-LIME FIZZES

makes 12

This creative cocktail is a fun take on the Boilermaker classically made with beer and a shot of tequila, whiskey, or vodka. We sweetened it up with citrus soda and lemonade concentrate for an extra-refreshing drink that's great for the beach!

1 (12 ounce) can frozen lemonade concentrate
2 cups silver tequila
1 (1.8 fluid ounce) bottle of lager, such as Stella Artois
1 (12 ounce) can lemon-lime soda

GARNISH

$^1/_4$ cup honey
Zest of 2 limes
$^1/_2$ cup granulated sugar

1. Place frozen lemonade concentrate into a punch bowl filled with ice. Stir in tequila, beer, and soda.
2. Pour honey onto a small shallow dish and it spread around. In another small shallow dish, toss to combine lime zest and sugar. Rim each glass with a thin layer of honey, followed by the lime-sugar mixture.
3. Ladle small amounts of the tequila mixture into each glass and serve.

Mini cocktail glasses and half-size tumblers are an elegant way to serve the perfect amount of buzz.

Cozy EGGNOG SHOOTERS

makes 12

When the days start getting shorter and colder, whip up these creamy little drinks to brighten your spirits.

2 egg yolks
1/4 cup granulated sugar
1 cup milk,* whole or low fat
1/2 cup cream
3/4 cup sweet bourbon, such as Maker's Mark
2 egg whites

GARNISH

1/4 cup honey
1/2 cup granulated sugar
1 tablespoon plus 1/2 teaspoon cinnamon, divided

**Substitute soy or almond milk to make yummy dairy-free nog.*

1. Place egg yolks into a stand mixer fitted with a paddle attachment (or use a hand mixer) and beat until light and fluffy. Add sugar and continue to beat, scraping down sides of the bowl. Stir in milk and cream. Pour mixture into a saucepan over medium-low heat and cook, stirring frequently, for 5 minutes, or until slightly thickened. Strain through a fine sieve and place over an ice bath to cool completely. Place mixture in the refrigerator and chill for an hour.
2. Remove chilled mixture from the refrigerator and stir in bourbon.
3. Using a stand mixer fitted with a whisk attachment, beat egg whites together until stiff peaks form, about 3 minutes. Fold egg whites into the chilled yolk mixture until completely combined and smooth.
4. Pour honey onto a small shallow plate and spread it around. In another small shallow dish, toss to combine sugar and 1 tablespoon of the cinnamon. Rim each glass with a thin layer of honey followed by the cinnamon-sugar. Ladle eggnog into each glass and serve topped with a sprinkle of cinnamon.

SUPPLIES

You don't need crazy culinary equipment to make delicious eats on a miniature scale. But having a few good tools makes tiny food preparation a breeze. These indispensable kitchen supplies are some of our favorites:

1. Wooden cutting board
2. Mini tart tin
3. Mini cake pan
4. Wooden spoon
5. Rubber spatula
6. Liquid measuring cups
7. Mixing bowl
8. Dry measuring cups
9. Piping tips
10. Parchment paper
11. Mini corn stick tin
12. Serving platters
13. Paring knife
14. Mini skewers
15. Measuring spoons
16. Baking sheet
17. Cocktail forks
18. Melon baller

EQUIVALENTS

Use these rounded equivalents to convert between the traditional American systems used to measure volume and weight and the metric system.

VOLUME

AMERICAN	IMPERIAL	METRIC
1/4 teaspoon		1.25 milliliters
1/2 teaspoon		2.5 milliliters
1 teaspoon		5 milliliters
1 tablespoon		7.5 milliliters
1/4 cup (4 tablespoons)	2 fluid ounces	15 milliliters
1/3 cup (5 tablespoons)	2 1/2 fluid ounces	60 milliliters
1/2 cup (8 tablespoons)	4 fluid ounces	75 milliliters
2/3 cup (10 tablespoons)	5 fluid ounces	125 milliliters
3/4 cup (12 tablespoons)	6 fluid ounces	150 milliliters
1 cup (16 tablespoons)	8 fluid ounces	175 milliliters
1 1/4 cups	10 fluid ounces	250 milliliters
1 1/2 cups	12 fluid ounces	300 milliliters
1 pint (2 cups)	16 fluid ounces	350 milliliters

OVEN TEMPERATURES

	°F	°C	GAS MARK
Very cool	250–275	130–140	1/2–2
Cool	300	148	2
Warm	325	163	3
Medium	350	177	4
Medium hot	375–400	190–204	5–6
Hot	425	218	7
Very hot	450–500	232–245	8–9

WEIGHTS

AMERICAN	METRIC
1/4 ounce	7 grams
1/2 ounce	15 grams
1 ounce	30 grams
2 ounces	55 grams
3 ounces	85 grams
4 ounces (1/4 pound)	110 grams
5 ounces	140 grams
6 ounces	170 grams
7 ounces	200 grams
8 ounces (1/2 pound)	225 grams
9 ounces	250 grams
10 ounces	280 grams
11 ounces	310 grams
12 ounces (3/4 pound)	340 grams
13 ounces	370 grams
14 ounces	400 grams
15 ounces	425 grams
16 ounces (1 pound)	450 grams

INDEX

ACKNOWLEDGMENTS

BIG THANKS to Adam Pearson and Matt Armendariz: You guys are the best mentors/teachers/people two girls could ask for. To Krystina Castella, for being such a great informative guide. To Alexandra Tumbas, for the fake laugh lesson. To Suzy Kil, for dealing with two very fussy girls and making us pretty. To our graphic designer, Katie Hatz, and our editor, Margaret McGuire: Thank you for your support through this whole process! **TERI** would like to thank David Lampert, Adrianna Adarme, Miki Swarthout, and John Gillilan. You will never understand how much your support means to me. I love you all so much. Thank you for always talking me out of going to the dark side. To my mom and Don: You taught me well, love you. To my dad and Lori, thank you for being understanding and supportive. To my sisters, thank you for being so special and so strange. Team Penny. And thanks to my grandparents and my aunt, I love you all so much. **JENNY** would like to thank Mom and Dad for your unconditional love and support and for teaching me the importance of humility, generosity, and never compromising my values. To Anne, my role model, mentor, and truly the greatest sister a person could have, for always bearing with me while I raid your closet, for patiently sitting back and listening to my weird daily rants, and for giving me the confidence to believe in myself. To Jwods, my best friend, beloved taste tester, and favorite funny man, for putting up with my inability to say no to anything Dexti, reality television, and Red Bulls. Your perpetual jokes, questionable dance moves, love, and support keep me moving with a smile on my face every day. I love you! To my lovely ladies, you're all so wonderfully exciting and weird. I wouldn't be nearly half the freak I am today without each and every one of you, and I love you all to death for it!

Psst . . .

WE'RE THROWING A TINY FOOD PARTY, AND YOU'RE INVITED!

Where:	QuirkBooks.com/TinyFoodParty
When:	Now
Why:	Because it's fun, and you can • *download menus for themed Tiny Food Parties* • *download templates for tiny party decorations* • *share photos from your own Tiny Food Party* • *join the conversation* *And much more!*